The People of Kenya and Uganda

Godfrey Mwakikagile

The People of Kenya and Uganda

Godfrey Mwakikagile

First Edition

ISBN 9789987160402

New Africa Press
Dar es Salaam, Tanzania

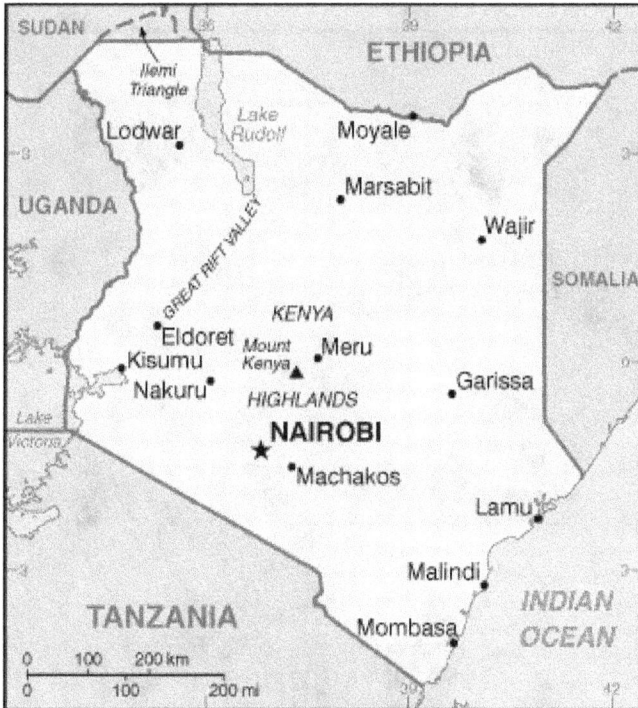

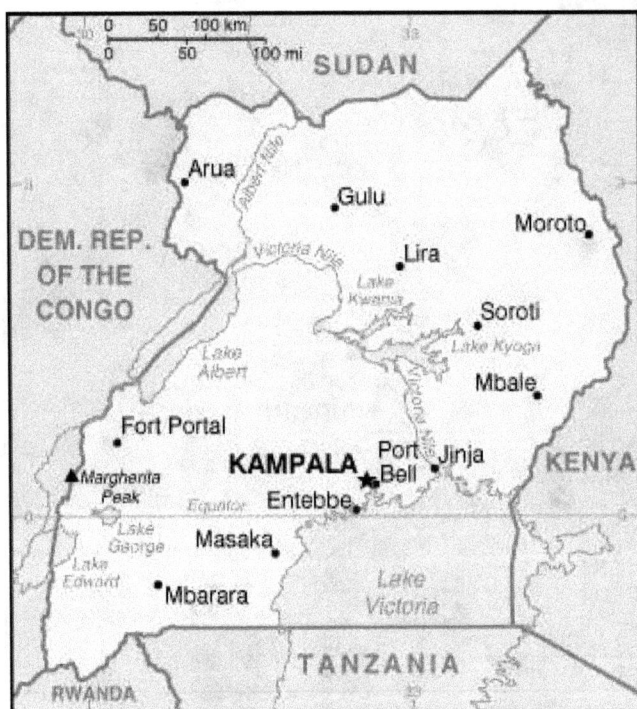

Introduction

THIS work focuses on the people of Kenya and Uganda as ethnic entities.

The cultural and ethnic diversity is one of the most fascinating features of the two countries which are also some of the most studied on the continent.

The groups are ethnocultural and linguistic in terms of identity. They are also historical entities, each with its own precolonial history. But in many cases, they also share a common history in terms of formation and cultural evolution through conquest, assimilation and integration. Many of them are a product of tribal and cultural integration.

Although they are separate with distinct identities, they share a common identity, as Kenyans and as Ugandans, as a result of colonial rule which united them to form the two countries.

This work is also an abridged and simplified version of my previous work, *Uganda: The and Its People*.

The part on Uganda focuses exclusively on the country's ethnic groups unlike the other book which covers other subjects as well. It is, simply, a survey of the different ethnic groups which collectively constitute Uganda as a nation.

The work does not pretend to be scholarly or deep in terms of details and analysis as my previous work on Uganda has been described by some people.

It only serves as a general introduction and is intended to introduce the people of Kenya and Uganda to those who know nothing or very little about them.

The people of Kenya

BLACK AFRICAN ethnic groups in Kenya are divided into three linguistic categories: Bantu, Nilotic, and Cushite. The Bantu constitute the majority. They include the Kikuyu, the Kamba, and the Luhya who are also among the five largest ethnic groups in the country.

The Kikuyu, the Luhya, the Kamba, the Meru, the Embu and the Gusii (Kisii) constitute the majority of the Bantu in Kenya. And they are mostly farmers like most Bantus are. But many of them also own cattle.

The Kikuyu homeland is around Mount Kenya and it is believed they arrived in the area in the 1700s.

There are many theories concerning their origin. Some say they migrated from Mozambique; others say from Congo.

What is clear from archaelogical and linguistic evidence is that they arrived in East Africa about 2,000 years ago from West Africa, especially from the Nigeria/Cameroon border area, as did the rest of the Bantu-speaking people, and their language belongs to the Niger-Congo family.

They have interacted with their neighbours the Maasai for a long time. The Maasai usually raided the Kikuyu for cattle and women, and the Kikuyu fought back. But in spite of all that, the two groups built strong commercial ties through the years and their people have been intermarrying almost from the time they first came into contact in central Kenya.

Another major Bantu ethnic group, the Kamba, also has an interesting history. It is said the Kamba migrated from what is now western Tanzania, a region occupied by the Nyamwezi ethnic group, one of the largest in Tanzania; implying that they were part of the Nyamwezi or are related to them. They moved east to the Usambara Mountains in northeastern Tanzania and eventually found their way to a semi-arid region in eastern Kenya which became their new home.

Other researchers contend that the Kamba are a product of many ethnic groups who intermarried and ended up creating a new ethnic group.

Whatever the case, it is generally believed that they arrived in their present homeland east of Nairobi towards the Tsavo National Park about 200 years ago.

The Kamba today are one of the most successful groups in Kenya, and one of the most well-known in East Africa.

In the past, they had a reputation as excellent traders, carrying on trade from the coast all the way to Lake Victoria, and all the way up to Lake Turkana. They traded in ivory, honey, weapons, beer, and ornaments.

They also excelled in barter, exchanging goods for food with their neighbours the Maasai and the Kikuyu. It was a matter of survival. They could not always produce much since their home region was arid or semi-arid land, forcing them to find food elsewhere.

And during colonial rule, the British "respected" them for their intelligence. They also had a reputation as fighters, another quality the British liked since they could use them as soldiers and as policemen. Many Kambas were conscripted into the army and fought in both world wars.

Even today, many Kambas serve in the armed forces and in law enforcement.

The Luhya are another major Bantu ethnic group in Kenya. Although successful, they have had to contend with problems of high population density through the years in a region where there is not enough fertile land for all the people.

The Meru and the Embu are the other Bantu ethnic groups in Kenya. They are related to the Kikuyu and are essentially farmers. They grow coffee, tea, maize, potatoes and pyrethrum as well as other crops. The Embu are also well-known for their honey and for dancing on stilts.

Then there are the Nilotic-speaking people as a major linguistic category in Kenya besides the Bantu.

The Nilotic group includes the Luo, the third largest ethnic group in the country. Other Nilotic-speaking groups include the Maasai, the Turkana, the Samburu, and the Kalenjin.

Originally, the Luo were pastoralists. But they changed their way of life when rinderpest killed their cows and became farmers and fishermen. Their involvement in fishing was facilitated by their geographical proximity to Lake Victoria in their new home region after they migrated from Sudan via Uganda. Some of them came straight from Sudan.

Like the Kikuyu, the Luo also played a major role in the independence struggle. Some of the most prominent Luo politicians of national and international statures include former Vice President Oginga Odinga, Minister of Economic Planning Tom Mboya, Foreign Affairs Minister Dr. Robert Ouko, and independence leader Achieng Oneko.

And the most prominent Luo outside Kenya and Africa is United States Senator of Barack Obama of Illinois. His father, also named Barack Obama after whom his son was named, earned a Ph.D. in economic from Harvard University and returned to Kenya where he served under

President Jomo Kenyatta.

He was one of the hundreds of Kenyan students who went to school in the United States on scholarships on the famous Tom Mboya Airlift in 1959.

Another Nilotic group, the Kalenjin, has an interesting history in terms of identity. The Kalenjins are actually a collection of related ethnic groups who speak the same language. They include the Kipsigis, renowned worldwide as long-distance runners; the Nandi, the Tugen and the Elyogo. President Daniel arap Moi was a Tugen.

The Kalenjin were once mainly pastoralists like the vast majority of the Nilotic-speaking people. And many of them still are today. But they are also engaged in agriculture in their fertile home region, the Rift Valley Province.

Besides the Luo, the most well-known Nilotic-speaking Kenyans are the Maasai, followed by the Turkana and the Samburu. The Maasai, who also came from Sudan like the most Nilotic-speaking peoples in Kenya, Tanzania and Uganda, are a small minority in both Kenya and Tanzania but are known worldwide because of their lifestyle and reputation as warriors.

They are also fiercely proud of their culture and way of life and have strongly resisted external pressure – including pressure from some national leaders – to change and adopt the "modern" way of life, which is a euphemism for the "Western" way of life.

They own not only cows but also goats. But cows are their most important possession in theie social, political and economic life.

There are two ethnic groups closely related to the Maasai: the Samburu and Turkana.

The traditional homeland of the Samburu is around Maralal in northern-central Kenya, an arid region. Like the Maasai, they also have the *morani*, the yung warriors; also like the Maasai, they prefer red blankets and use red ochre to paint their heads. The women wear beads. And like the

Maasai, they also own cows and goats, with the cows being their most important possession and the centre of their social, political and economic life.

Unlike some Nilotic-speaking people who have adopted other ways of life to adjust to new realities, the Samburu have remained pastoralist, preferring a nomadic way of life. When pasture becomes scarce in their arid and semi-arid homeland, they pack up and go, taking their *manyata* (portable houses and other essential items) on their camels to find better pastures. This is similar to what Somalis do. But they are not related. The Somali are Cushitic.

The other major Nilotic-speaking group is the Turkana. The Turkana have a reputation as fierce fighters, just like their kith-and-kin the Maasai and the Samburu. They own other animals besides cows. They have goats, sheep, and camels, but cow ownership is still the most important aspect of their social, political and economic life. They live in an arid region near Lake Turkana.

And all three – the Maasai, the Samburu and the Turkana – are cattle rustlers. The government has not been able to stop them and law enforcement officials usually leave them alone. Disputes among them are settled by their elders. They were colonised like the rest of the Africans but the colonial rulers failed to conquer them in one fundamental respect: their way of life which has remained intact for hundreds of years.

The other major lingustic group is the Cushitic. The Cushites are a minority in Kenya and live mostly in the North Eastern Province which borders Somalia and Ethiopia. They include the Somali, the Boran, the El Molo, the Burji Dassenich, the Gabbra, the Orma, the Sakuye, the Boni, the Wata, the Yaaka, the Daholo, the Rendille, and the Galla.

The Somali and the Galla are the most well-known. But it is the Somali who are the dominant group in the region. They own cattle, goats, sheep, and camels in the arid and inhospitable region of northern Kenya and lead a nomadic way of life in search of water and pasture for their herds. They also have a reputation as fierce fighters.

The Swahili are some of the most well-known people in East Africa, especially in Kenya and Tanzania, but they don't constitute an ethnic group the way they Kikuyu or the Luo do. They are essentially a linguistic and cultural group, and a product of many tribes and non-indigenous groups especially the Arabs. They live mostly along the coast.

Also most of the Arabs live along the coast. They are one of the three main non-indigenous groups in Kenya, the other ones being Asian and British.

Most Arabs speak Swahili rather than Arabic and see themselves as Africans, not as citizens of the Arab world. Most Arabs in Kenya are Kenyan citizens.

There are also many Arabs in Kenya who are not Kenyans. They come mainly from Yemen and are small traders. They are commonly known as *Washihiri* or simply *Shihiri*, but mostly as *Washihiri* in Kiswahili; a term also applied to them in neighbouring Tanzania.

The British are also a significant minority and Kenya has one of the largest European communities in Africa. Kenyans of British descent include members of the aristocracy. And many of them continue to have great influence in the country especially among the elite including national leaders.

Kenyans of Asian descent, commonly known as Indians, are the most prosperous group in Kenya – and the rest of East Africa – besides the British and other whites who have always been on top.

The term "Indian" is collectively used to identify Pakistanis as well, although the majority of the Asians in Kenya came from India.

India and Pakistan were one country until 1947 and most of the immigrants in East Africa today immigrated to the region before Indian independence in 1947 when the sub-continent was split into India and Pakistan.

So, in a way, the term "Indian" is the appropriate designation even for those who came from Pakistan. They all came from the Indian sub-continent as a geographical entity.

The prosperity of Indians in Kenya and other parts of Africa has been a source of resentment towards them among many black Africans. But the resentment is also attributed to the mistreatment of the indigenous people whom the majority of Indians see as inferior to them.

It is raw-naked racism even if one may argue that they are clannish more than anything else. Indians are both clannish and racist; a fact acknowledged even by some Indians themselves who admit that black Africans are exploited and mistreated by them.

And social interaction as equals between the two is almost totally out of the question. It is also extremely rare for black Africans and Indians to intermarry. Where such unions have taken place, mostly illicit relationships, it has been between Indian men and black African women. Black men dating Indian girls or women, let alone marrying them, is considered virtually taboo by most Indians, although there have been a number cases where this taboo has been broken.

Marriage within the "clan," that is, within the Indian - or Asian community as it is also called, is strictly enforced almost with religious zeal and devotion. And anyone who defies that risks ostracisation.

However, many Indians are tolerant of marriage with whites – and even accept it whether or not it involves Indian women and white men. The biggest concern has been about non-Indians, especially blacks, dating or marrying Indian women.

The willingness of Indians to accept unions between whites and Indians has only reinforced the belief and vindicated the claim of those who say Asians are racist towards blacks more than anybody else.

In spite of the poor race relations between Indians and black Africans in Kenya and other African countries, there is no question that vast majority of Indians consider Africa to be home.

This was clearly demonstrated in the late sixties and in the seventies when many Indians left Tanzania and Kenya for India with the intention of living there permanently. They said they were returning to their homeland. And they did in large numbers.

But they couldn't fit in and returned to East Africa despite the fact that India was their ancestral homeland. That is because they were African more than anything else. India was the home of their ancestors, not theirs. They were born and brought up in East Africa, as were their parents and grandparents in many cases, and were therefore East Africans, not Indians of India.

After looking at the major ethnic and linguistic groups in the country, we now turn our attention to some of the other groups which are numerically smaller but no less important as an integral part of Kenya.

The Bajuni are among those groups. They are a small ethnic group in the Coast Province. They live mostly in northern Kenya. Some of them also live in southern Somalia. And they are mostly fishermen and sailors. But they are also involved in other economic activities including metalwork. They speak a language which is basically Kiswahili, or Swahili, although they call their version Kibajuni.

The word Kibajuni is also a Kiswahili term. Ki- is a prefix in Kiswahili applied to all languages. Thus, the Kikuyu speak Kikuyu, the Kamba, Kikamba, and the Luo, Kiluo. It goes on and on.

The Bajuni call themselves and are known as Wabajuni; which is another Swahili or Kiswahili term. Wa- is a prefix denoting collective identity. The Kikuyu are called Wakikuyu in Kiswahili; the Meru are called Wameru; the Somali are called Wasomali; and Swahili are called Waswahili.

The Bukusu don't constitute a distinct ethnic entity but are a sub-ethnic group of the Luhya. There are 17 such sub-groups which collectively constitute the Luhya ethnic group.

The Bukusu are therefore an example of many other groups in Kenya which are not considered by some people to be tribes or separate ethnic groups but sub-tribes. But they are the largest sub-group in the Luhya ethnic entity which some people call the Luhya "nation."

The Luhya is called a "nation" - mostly by the Luhya themselves - mainly because of its size; the same thing which could be applied to other large ethnic groups such as the Kikuyu, the Luo and the Kamba.

The Nandi, although a sub-group of the Kalenjin, are considered to be a separate tribe just like the other Kalenjin sub-groups – the Turkana and the Kipsigis. They live mostly in the highland areas of the Nandi Hills in the Rift Valley Province and have a reputation as fighters like their brethren, the other Kalenjins. They are farmers and cattle-herders.

The Pokot are also Kalenjin but a distinct group. They live in West Pokot District and Baringo District. They are found in in eastern Uganda. In Karamoja District. They also have a reputation as fierce fighters as most Nilotic-speaking tribes do. They are both farmers and pastoralists, usually depending on where they live. The Hill Pokot live in the highlands and are farmers; while the Plains Pokot in the dry and infertile plains own livestock – cattle, sheep, and goats.

The Gusii, also known as Kisii, are Bantu and live in Kisii (Gusii) District in Nyanza Province in western Kenya whose dominant group is the Nilotic Luo.

They are isolated as a Bantu group in the sense that they are surrounded by Nilotic-speaking tribes – the Luo, the Maasai, the Kipsigis, and the Nandi – who traditionally have been hostile towards them. As a result,

17

they became tough fighters themselves in order to be able to defend themselves against the Nilotic cattle raiders.

The Kisii live in a very fertile hilly district where they grow a lot of tea, coffee, bananas and other crops. But there is shortage of land and many Kisii have migrated to other parts of Kenya.

The Kisii are also one of the largest ethnic groups in Kenya. They rank fifth after the Kamba who are preceded by the Kikuyu, the Luhya, and the Luo.

All the largest ethnic groups in Kenya are Bantu – Kikuyu, Luhya, Kamba, and Kisii – except the Luo who rank third; they used to be second in numerical until they were surpassed by the Luhya.

The Kuria straddle the Kenyan-Tanzanian border close to Lake Victoria. They are found in Mara Region in northern Tanzania – which is also the home region of former Tanzanian President Julius Nyerere who was a member of the Zanaki tribe in Musoma District, Mara Region – and in Nyanza Province.

The Digo are another ethnic group found in both Kenya and Tanzania. They are a Bantu group and live along the coast in both countries between Mombasa in southern Kenya and Tanga in northern Tanzania. The majority of them live in Kenya.

The Orma live in southeastern Kenya mostly along the lower Tana River. They are also called Galla, a term commonly used in Ethiopia to identify the same ethnic group.

They are semi-nomadic and move from their southeastern desert homes only during the rainy season when they go inland in search of pastures for their livestock.

The Oromo are found mostly in Ethiopia but also in Kenya and Somalia in smaller numbers. In fact, they are the largest ethnic group in Ethiopia. They are Cushitic.

They are also one of the largest Cushitic-speaking ethnic groups in Eastern and Northeastern Africa which includes the Horn of Africa. And their physical features, and language as well as culture, clearly distinguishes them from Bantu and Nilotic groups in Kenya, pointing to their "origin" in the Horn of Africa. The Orma or Galla are related to them.

The Pokomo are a Bantu group who live along the Tana River in the Tana River District and are mostly farmers.

The Rendille are one of the groups which are considered to be on the verge of extinction unless something is done to save them from this catastrophe.

They are nomadic pastoralists and live in the Kaisut Desert. in Northern Kenya where they roam on their camels with their livestock which is the main source of sustenance. Meat and milk are a main part of their diet.

Another group that is considered to be a part of another tribe yet is distinct from that tribe and has its own identity is the Samburu which we earlier briefly looked at.

They are related to the Maasai. And they call themselves Lokop or Loikop. And they speak the Samburu language, not Maasai.

But like the Maasai, they part of the Maa speaking people. And about 95 per cent of the words of both languages – Samburu and Maasai – are the same, showing that they indeed basically the same people.

In fact, even the name Samburu is of Maasai origin and comes from the word *samburi* which is a leather bag used by the Samburu to carry a variety of items. But, for whatever reason, they acquired their own ethnic identity. Some people have attributed this to the colonial rulers who sometimes divided people to "create" different ethnic groups for administrative purposes and to facilitate colonial rule.

They are also said to have multiple origins, although all related. Some Samburu are descended from the Maasai, and others from the Turkana, Borana (also called Boran), and Rendille. And all these are Nilotic groups.

19

Although they own mainly cattle, they also have sheep, goats and camels as an important of their livestock in an arid region which forces them to have a large number of animals many of which don't survive because of the harsh climate.

Samburu District was once a large part of the Northern Frontier District (NFD) - as the region was called before and a few years after independence - which is now the North Eastern Province. It was isolated for all practical purposes and only government officials were allowed to enter the region.

It was closed to foreigners and one had to get a special permit to enter the Northern Frontier District. Even today, Samburu District is a remote, harsh area.

Like the Maasai, they also came from Sudan. And they are more conservative – much more traditional in life and attitude – than their cousins the Maasai; which is quite a distinction since the Maasai themselves are known for their stiff resistance to alien influences.

The Taveta are a Bantu ethnic group who live in south-central Kenya. They are called Wataveta in Kiswahili, and call themselves that, and their language – also in Kiswahili – is known as Kitaveta.

There are also elements of other tribes in the Tavetan population, especially the Taita, the Kamba, the Maasai, and the Chaga. The Chaga are a tribe in northeastern Tanzania in Kilimanjaro Region on the southern and southeastern slopes of Mount Kilimanjaro and throughout Moshi District.

TheTaveta live mostly between the Tsavo National Park and the Tanzanian border and are mostly subsistence farmers. Some of them also work on local sisal plantations and are engaged in other economic activities.

The Yaaku are of Cushitic origin but gave up their original language and now speak a Maasai variant known as Mukogodo-Maasai. They were assimilated by the Maasai but some words from their old Yaaku language are

20

a part of their vocabulary today.

They live in the Mukogodo forest west of Mount Kenya, which is a division of the Laikipia District in the Rift Valley Province, and were once hunter-gatherers and bee-keepers. They eventually adopted the Maasai pastoralist culture, although some of them are still bee-keepers.

They now consider themselves to be a sub-tribe of the Maasai, and are indeed Maasai in terms of language and culture. All the old people who spoke the original Yaaku language are dead.

Tragically, the Yaaku are some of the people who have lost their original language and culture due to assimilation, a fate that has befallen other indigenous groups in different parts of the world with dire consequences: loss of identity, turning them into carbon copies, poor carbon copies, of other people.

It is a tragic loss.

Indigenous cultures in Kenya

A FUSION of cultures through the centuries has produced a synthesis that is uniquely Kenyan. And it is the local component – African tribes and their cultures found only in Kenya – that has given this cultural blend or amalgam its unique character.

It has been a confluence of cultures, flowing for centuries from Asia and the Middle East, and later from Europe, mingling with African cultures not only in Kenya but in other parts of East Africa, especially neighbouring Tanzania. And it has been one of the most exciting events, and one of the most enriching experiences, in the history of human interaction.

But while all these foreign cultures spread to other parts of the region besides Kenya, during the same period, they did not produce exactly the same synthesis when they fused with local cultures because the tribes found in Tanzania, for example, are not the same tribes that are found in Kenya except a few like the Maasai and the Digo found in both countries; and the Luo found in Kenya, Uganda and Tanzania.

Each of these cultural and linguistic groups found in Kenya has its own way of life that has persisted through the centuries. Some of these groups form clusters. And it is these groups and their different ways of life which we are going to focus on in this chapter to get some understanding of the African way of life in this East African country.

Some of the most fascinating cultures have evolved in the mountainous regions of Kenya and geography has had a profound influence on their evolution. As Godfrey Mwakikagile, a writer from neighbouring Tanzania, states in his book *Africa and The West*:

(A) diversity of cultures (in Africa)...evolved through the centuries as a result of migrations which necessitated adaptation to new environments. Such evolution of cultures and customs also reflects the nature of the new environments including geography. For example, Mount Kenya would not have figured prominently in Kikuyu customs had there been no Mount Kenya in the area where the Kikuyu settled. - (Godfrey Mwakikagile, *Africa and The West* (Huntington, New York: Nova Science Publishers, Inc.,), p. 12).

It means the Kikuyu would have found another point of reference or a geographical feature of cultural relevance and religious significance – based on their beliefs – had there been no such mountain.

It could have been a lake, a valley, or even a desert, and would still have served the same purpose as Mount Kenya does today as the home of the Kikuyu god, *Ngai*, and which they face when they pray as Jomo Kenyatta eloquently stated in his study of Kikuyu culture, customs and beliefs appropriately entitled, *Facing Mount Kenya* first published in 1938.

According to Kikuyu beliefs, all creation began at the summit of Mount Kenya. The snow-capped peak of the mountain is the creator's dwelling place.

The Kikuyu believe that *Ngai*, whom they say is the supreme creator, came down from the heavens to his

24

mountainous throne to survey his newly created lands. The mountain became *Kirinyaga*, his resting place, and it was from here that he called forth Gikuyu, the father of the Kikuyu people.

It is a rough equivalent of the Biblical account of creation and the Kikuyu may or may not have appropriated some concepts from the Bible and incorporated them into their beliefs through the years, although this is highly unlikely since they had their own system of belief, already well-established, long before Christianity was introduced to them.

The Kikuyu believe *Ngai* told Gikuyu, the father of the Kikuyu people, or the Kikuyu nation, that all the lands around Kirinyaga would be the home of Gikuyu and his children forever.

The Kikuyu belief in *Ngai* as their creator also says that *Ngai* sent Gikuyu to a grove of fig trees where he found a woman called Mumbi who became his wife.

The grove of fig trees came to be known as *Mukuru wa Nyagathanga*, which means the birthplace of all Kikuyus. And it is still revered by the Kikuyu today as a sacred place and as an integral part of their very being, heart and soul.

The Kikuyu also sacrifice a goat beneath a fig tree as an offering to their god, *Ngai*, in times of drought when they pray for rain.

When the Kikuyu migrated to the central highlands of Kenya, they came into contact with Maasai with whom they shared some traditional practices including the way they dressed, in some respects. A lot of intermarriage between the members of the two tribes also took place.

The intermarriage led to the integration of some Maasai clans into the Kikuyu nation of which they became an integral part indistinguishable from the Kikuyu themselves. It was total integration and assimilation, and the dominant culture after this absorption of the Maasai took place was Kikuyu.

25

Although some elements of foreign cultures which have become a part of the Kikuyu way of life, for example Western civilisation, there is still a very strong sense of commitment to the traditional way of life – in terms of values - among many Kikuyus including educated ones. And they have always remained bound by strict and strong ties of clan loyalty and an even stronger sense of tribal unity traced all the way back to the time when their nation came into being. This is a very important part of Kikuyu culture.

Unfortunately, it also fosters tribalism in a heterogeneous society like Kenya. And that is one of the reasons why tribalism is so entrenched in this country of about 50 ethnic groups. And as the dominant tribe in Kenya, the Kikuyu have played a prominent role in sustaining tribalism across the spectrum.

Yet, it can also be explained in terms of their culture and origin as a people who are supposed to stick together and who see themselves as one, with a common ancestry, descended from Gikuyu and Mumbi, their original parents. They all belong to one family, *Nyumba ya Mumbi*, which literally means the house of Mumbi as the mother of the Kikuyu nation.

The Kikuyu have nine clans and their society is strongly patriarchal. And traditional ceremonies involving rites of passage – initiation and marriage – are a very important part of the Kikuyu way of life even among urban dwellers even there are those who may shun them and see them as "primitive" and "backward" practices.

Besides Mount Kenya and its cultural and religious significance for the Kikuyu, another important mountain in the country is Mount Elgon.

It also has important cultural and historical significance for the people who live around it.

Long before Europeans came, the mountain had deep caves in which herds of cattle could be hidden and protected. Great piles of grain were also stored in the caves.

The original inhabitants around this area looked like Maasais in terms of physical appearance. In fact, for a long time, many people thought they were indeed Maasai. But they were not.

They were members of four very small tribes known as the Kony, the Sapei, the Pok, and the Bungomek. They are still there today and are collectively known as the Saboat. They are a part of the Kalenjin, which itself is a collection of related tribes.

There is a strong cultural affinity among the Kalenjin and the Saboat have the strongest ties with the Nandi in terms of culture.

The Saboat called the mountain, Masop, and made excellent use of this mountainous area. It was perfect for their needs. They grew crops on the mountain slopes, and they also had livestock, especially cows.

They knew about the caves in what is now called Mount Elgon and used them as granaries and stables for their livestock. The caves were also an excellent place of refuge for the Saboat during inter-tribal wars. They also protected them from bad weather.

Mount Elgon also provided them with much-needed salt. The salt was in the caves. Elephants would make trips to the caves every night to scrape the walls with their tasks and lick the salt which fell to the ground. Then the Saboat would go to the caves to collect some of the salt after the elephants were gone and use it to preserve their food.

Hunting was also common in Saboat culture. Even elephants were hunted. The Saboat used pit traps at the entrance of the caves to catch them.

Besides the Saboat, there is another group of people, the Teso, to whom Mount Elgon is very important.

They come from the Karamajong region in Uganda. No one is exactly sure if they are descended from the Karamajong, a Ugandan tribe, but they do have strong cultural and linguistic ties to the region which includes

Mount Elgon in this border area where Kenya and Uganda share a common boundary.

They have been influenced by neighbouring tribes through the years, absorbing some of their cultural elements and practices. Some of the people who have influenced them are the Luo but they have closest ties with the Pokot, a Kalenjin tribe found throughout western Laikipia and the area north of the Cherangani Hills.

It is these cultural ties between the Pokot and the Teso which separate the Pokot - or distinguishes them - from the rest of the Kalenjin tribes. But there is one major difference between the two groups.

For a long time, the Pokot have had two distinct tribal units: nomadic cattle herders and farmers. By remarkable contrast, the Teso were originally farmers who recently became cattle herders.

The culture of the Teso is defined by its age system, and respect for elders is extremely important as it is in all African cultures. Traditionally, power in a Teso clan and in the tribe itself comes from seniority. It is vested in older people.

Initiation is also a very important part of Teso culture but traditionally it was not through circumcision – a practice the Teso adopted from the Karamajong – but through animal sacrifice and big feasts that young men were initiated into manhood.

The Teso also had a strong belief in divining and prophecy and it is still a very important part of their culture even today.

Traditional diviners, called *emuron*, cast sandals on the ground and, depending on how they fall, read their positions to tell the future and detect signs for things to come. It is also a common religious practice in the traditional beliefs of other northern Kenyan tribes such as the Pokot, the Samburu, and the Borana (or Boran).

With its location on the Kenyan-Ugandan border, Mount Elgon serves as some sort of "cultural" bond between the tribes on both sides of the border which share many cultural traits.

Both the Saboat in Kenya and the Teso in Uganda have many bonds and cultural ties to Eastern Ugandan tribes, and Mount Elgon has figured prominently in their history. The boundary between the two countries has done little to sever those ties

Roughly in the same region are the Western Highlands. It is an area of great cultural significance and the highlands once served as a meeting point for two ethnic groups.

The area was originally inhabited by a Cushitic people who migrated from southern Ethiopia. Then came Nilotic tribes from southern Sudan and Uganda who settled in the same region. The result was intermariage between these two groups, producing a synthesis of cultures we see today.

The cultures which evolved in these highlands, with their Nilotic and Cushitic content, remain separate from other Nilotic – Maasai, Samburu, and Luo – and Cushitic cultures. The other Cushitic cultures referred to here which are separate from the Cushitic cultures in the highlands include the Gabbra, and Boran Oromo.

The ones in the Western Highlands are distinct from them despite their common origin because of the cultural amalgamation that took place in those highlands between Nilotic and Cushitic cultures.

The cultures of the Western Highlands are sometimes identified as Highland Nilotes. The common name is Kalenjin.

The Kalenjin are united by a strong sense of community and rites of passage. This is a very important aspect of their culture. There is also a common belief among them in the not-so-distant past which said children were not members of the tribe. They became members only after they had been initiated.

One of the more well-known and bigger Kalenjin

groups is the Kipsigis. Traditionally, they had an elaborate and extensive system of clans, and were socially centred around a unit called the *kokuet*.

It was a large collection of up to 60 family homesteads and was structured as an insurance and support unit, not just for economic needs but for social needs as well, including emotional support and other kinds of support across a wide range of spectrum.

The families relied on each other for support and assistance in times of need. And they still do so today in this deeply conservative society resistance to change and foreign influences.

The tribe which the Kipsigis are closely related to is the Nandi.

The traditional homeland of the Nandi was the Kapsabet region, while that of the Kipsigis was the area of Kericho where these former cattle herders turned to agriculture throughout the 20th century, growing tea and other crops, as they still do. And both tribes live in the same areas today as their traditional strongholds.

The social structure of the Nandi was and still is very similar to that of the Kipsigis. The collective homesteads of the Nandi are called *pororiet*.

Initiation has always been an important part of Nandi culture which is characterised by an age-set system. Young men who became warriors were initiated at a ceremony where a white bull was sacrificed, and much of the same practice goes on today.

The Nandi have always been great cattle raiders. Historically, they raided the Luo and the Maasai. They also attacked caravans of traders from the coast who went far into the interor to conduct business.

Their reputation as fierce fighters was enhanced when they took on the British who entered their territory in the early part of the 20th century. British forces were repeatedly repelled by Nandi warriors. It was not until after a five-year military campaign by British forces that the Nandi were finally subdued. But they went down in history with their reputation as fighters remaining intact, despite their loss.

The Nandi generally maintained cordial relations with the other Kalenjin groups with whom they shared cultural affinity. They included the Elgeyo and the Tugen who have always had a reputation as great farmers. Among the crops grown in the region were maize and millet, as they still are today. The tribes in the region also kept large herds of cattle, goats and sheep as they still do today.

Another Kalenjin tribe was the Marakwet living on Cherengani Hills. They shared many cultural traits with the other Kalenjin groups in the region. The Marakwet were made up of six clans. The name Cherengani for the hills comes from the name of one of the clans.

The Marakwet built terraced villages on the slopes of the hills, as they still do today, and goats remain the most common and most important animal members of this tribe like to keep for one very important reason: the goats are well adapted to life on the steep slopes of the Cherengani Hills.

Further south are the Kisii who probably migrated from Uganda. Unlike the rest of the people in the region, they are a Bantu group, therefore have a Bantu culture and share many cultural elements with other Bantu cultures.

When the Luo, a Nilotic group, migrated to the region from Sudan in the mid-500s, the Kisiss were forced to relocate.

Raids on the Kisii by the Maasai and the Kipsigis, both Nilotic like the Luo, also forced the Kisii to find a new home in the highlands where they continued to live as farmers. Even today, the highlands are considered to be their homeland. And their culture has evolved to suit the environment.

The Kisii have a reputation as great farmers and through the years have traded with the Luo, selling their agricultural products to them. The interaction has also led to an accommodation of cultures, and with some cultural elements flowing from both sides influencing each other in varying degrees.

Some of the most outstanding products of Kisii culture include wooden stools and different items of furniture. The Kisii, who have quite a reputation as excellent craftsmen in addition to their reputation as great farmers, also quarry and carve soapstone.

Another area of Kenya whose hills and mountains are inextricably linked with the culture of the people who live there is in the southern part of the country. It is the region of the Taita and Chyulu Hills, framing the vast plains of Tsavo and lying within view of Mount Kilimanjaro in neighbouring Tanzania.

The Chyulu hills form a border between the plains of Amboseli and the wilderness of Tsavo. This is also border country between Maasailand and Kambaland. And members of both tribes – the Maasai and the Kamba – are found throughout the area.

The Maasai graze their herds in this area. It is also here where the Kamba crossed the hills a long time ago when they migrated from the Usambara mountains in northeastern Tanzania after their long journey from what is now western Tanzania, their original homeland.

And both tribes share a common belief about the existence of *Shetani*, which means Satan or the Devil in Kiswahili, in the area. Many local people say the area is haunted by the ghosts of the people who died and got buried under the lava of these hills. A large lava flow took place in this area a long time ago and claimed many lives, according to local legend.

Many people in this area claim that mournful cries can be heard from under the ground at night, and have been known to leave offerings of food on the rocks to appease the departed souls trapped there.

The Taita Hills are the homeland of the Taita people. They are a well-established tribe in the region and are believed to have migrated from the northeastern coast of Kenya. During their long occupancy of the Taita Hills, they have developed a strong and unifying cultural character and the hills are very much an integral part of their lives, hence their culture.

The Taita are also some of Kenya's best farmers and are known as a strongly agricultural people. They have a long history of well-developed agriculture and have for years grown millet and sugar cane. They later started growing maize.

They also built highly developed systems of irrigation using hollowed sugar cane pipes. Water was transported fairly long distances, sometimes for about a mile. Cultivation entailed extensive clearance of land, with mean clearing the land, and the women cultivating and working the fields. That is how it was traditionally done according to their culture. And they still do it today.

They did not keep animals except only on a limited scale, and cow ownership is a relatively new practice among them. They started acquiring cattle only in the 20th century. But they were highly skilled in using iron, making agricultural implements and weapons.

The Taita had six traditional clans, named numerically in the order by which each group were believed to have migrated to the hills from northeastern Kenya.

Inter-clan ties were not particularly strong but they shared traditional customs which were unified, thus forming some kind of indissoluble bond among them.

Some of the caves in the Taita Hills have great cultural and religious significance. They are considered to be sacred and were used as a repository for ancestral skulls in keeping with their traditional religion of ancestor worship so common among many African tribes.

The departed ancestors are the living dead and act as intermediaries between the living the Creator. Ugandan scholar and Christian religious philosopher, Dr.John Mbiti, has addressed the subject of traditional worship in his excellent book, *African Religions and Philosophy*.

His book was seminal work and was the first to significantly challenge Christian assumptions that traditional African religions were demonic and anti-Christian. The Taita and other Africans who practice traditional beliefs are among those who agree with Professor Mbiti on this subject.

Besides the Taita, other people who live in the area of the Taita and Chyulu Hills are the members of the Taveta tribe. They live in the Taveta area and around Lakes Chala and Jipe.

They are not related to the Taita but they have cultural ties to both the Maasai and the Kamba who also live in the same region.

Equally important as the mountains as an integral part of culture of a number of Kenya's ethnic groups are the forests in this tropical country.

In fact, most of the forests in Kenya have some cultural significance; for example, those surrounding the sacred peak of Mount Kenya so important to the Kikuyu and related tribes, and the coastal forests surrounding the lost city-state of Gedi whose history also is of great cultural significance in terms of interaction between cultures, African and foreign, since Gedi was a product of those cultures.

There are the Aberdare mountains, simply known as the Aberdares, or Nyandarua in the Kikuyu language, which played a very important part in the history of Kenya as the sanctuary for the Mau Mau fighters during the struggle for independence.

Nyandarua is, among the Kikuyu, the name for a traditional rack for drying animal skins and hides, and the spine of the Aberdare range of mountains resembles this rack. The Kikuyu have long used the fertile slopes of the Aberdare range and it became a bone of contention between these indigenous people and the British settlers who wanted to turn Kenya into a "White Man's Country."

As the first governor of Kenya, Sir Charles Eliot, a retired soldier, emphatically stated in 1905 after seizing some of the most fertile land from the Kikuyu in the central highlands:

The Protectorate is a White Man's Country. This being so, it is mere hypocrisy not to admit that white interests must be paramount and that the main object of our policy and legislation should be to found a white colony. - (Charles Eliot, *The East African Protectorate* (London: Arnold, 1905), quoted by George Padmore, *Pan-Africanism or Communism? The Coming Struggle for Africa* (London: Denis Dobson, 1956), p. 233. See also Charles Eliot quoted by Godfrey Mwakikagile, *Africa and The West* (Huntington, New York: Nova Science Publishers, Inc.,), p. 10).

The Aberdares were named after Lord Aberdare who was president of the Royal Geographic Society.

The town of Nyeri, located east of the Aberdare mountains, was the centre of the "Happy Valley" settlers during colonial times. It was a group of British aristocrats and adventurers who became notorious for their decadent lifestyles and exploits in the 1930's and 1940's. Even today, the town brings back memories of life in the olden days.

It still has the atmosphere of a sleepy English village, an impression bolstered by the coll air and morning mists which reminded the settlers of life in Britain. It was very much a cultural centre for the British during colonial times.

Just outside of the town is the Outspan Hotel, a monument to a bygone era: how life was for the white settlers in colonial times. The hotel also is the base for visitors to Treetops, another monument to the past.

The Treetops is a very important part of British history. It was here, at the Treetops, where Queen Elizabeth II was staying on the night of February 6th 1952 when his father King George IV died and she had to fly back to England for the funeral and for the coronation as the new monarch.

It was at this forest lodge, which is surrounded by herds of buffalo and elephant, where Elizabeth officially marked her passage from princess to queen.

It was also during the same period that Mau Mau was in full swing and the Aberdares became a very important operational base and hiding place for the freedom fighters who played a critical role in speeding up the end of colonial rule in Kenya.

Today the Aberdares are a national park, and the surrounding slopes are farmland owned by the Kikuyu, the indigenous inhabitants of the area.

Another forest which is inextricably linked with the cultural life and identity of the people who live around it is the Kakamega Forest in western Kenya.

The people who live around this forest are Luhyas. Some live inside the forest and draw sustenance from it. The forest provides them with many things and has also played an important part in shaping the cultural life of the Luhya people in general.

They came from eastern Uganda and settled in Kenya during a period of major Bantu migration that lasted from 1570 to the mid-1600s. A number of factors contributed this migration: tribal conflicts, lack of land due to high population density in their original home in eastern Uganda, and sleeping sickness.

When they arrived in the area which later became a part of a country called Kenya, they found it to be very fertile. And it came to be known as *Buluhya*, as it still is today.

Given the fertile land and abundant rainfall, together with their skills as farmers, their new homeland was ideal for population growth and the establishment of a well-structured society. Their population grew, as did their influence in the region among other tribes, and they became some of the most successful people in Kenya.

And they are some of the most tradition-bound people in Kenya, as the structure of their society clearly shows.

They have a highly complex system of clans and sub-clans unlike many other tribes in the country.

Some studies show that they may have about 750 clans, which is a very large number.

The clan system formed the basis of the Luhya form of government which revolved around powerful clan leaders called *Omwami*. And it remains the foundation of Luhya society even today.

The large number of clans had its advantages: flexibility and diversity in the traditional way of life. The Luhya did not live under a rigid, highly centralised form of government so typical of so many countries across the continent during the post-colonial period when dictatorship became institutionalised on a continental scale, with very few exceptions such as Botswana.

With such great diversity, there was ample room for experimentation and adaptation, and for innovative ideas. Different Luhya clans had their own way of doing things and even had their own different customs not followed by other clans. And there were other differences in culture. It was basically the same Luhya culture, but with some differences among different clans.

And that is still the case today. There are many different Luhya traditions. Yet they are united as one people and follow the same practices in many areas of life. For example, all Luhya clans practise some form of male initiation. Yet the initiation rites vary from clan to clan, ranging from traditional circumcision to the removal of lower teeth.

There are other common rituals which bind the Luhya together as a homogeneous whole and as a single cultural entity despite variations within. The sacrifice of livestock is one of them. It is used to mark rites of passage including birth and marriage.

One of the most important Luhya practices may have been adopted from the Luo who are some of their neighbours: the ceremonial driving of cattle to funerals.

Bullfighting is one of the most well-known Luhya customs. Besides its cultural significance, it is also a very popular sport among the Luhya.

In addition to their reputation as great farmers, the Luhya have also been long known to be excellent builders and roof thatchers. But even the building of houses was based on the clan system, as it still is in many cases especially among those who still follow the traditional way of life and observe Luhya customs. Traditional villages, known as *Itala*, were a part of a larger association of clans called *olukongo* which still exists today among many Luhyas.

The Luhya have demonstrated their skills not only as excellent builders and farmers; they also produce excellent pottery. They are also excellent weavers.

The Luhya are also known for their spectacular traditional dances. One of the most popular daces is known as *sikuti*. It is performed by groups of paired men and women to the accompaniment of a cacophony of bells and whistles.

The Luhya live in a region surrounded by Nilotic tribes. They are therefore somewhat "isolated" as a Bantu group. But they have close relatives in the region, the Kuria, whose traditional homeland was in the southern part near the border of what is now Tanzania.

The Kuria are also found in Tanzania in the northern region of Mara which borders Kenya and are believed to have moved south from the foothills of Mount Elgon after the Bantu migration from Uganda which centuries before started in West Africa.

Although the Kuria migrated to Kenya from Uganda as part of the Luhya migrations, they eventually developed their own customs and established a highly ritualised community. They were known for decorating their bodies in a very spectacular way. They were also known for their highly rhythmic music and dance. Mysticism also played a major role in their lives and they were known for their

38

skills of prophecy and rainmaking.

Another tribe related to the Kuria, hence the Luhya as well, is the Kisii. Kisii folkrole speaks of shared ancestry not just with the Kuria and the Luhya but also with the Kikuyu, the Embu and the Meru.

And like the Luhya and the Kuria, the Kisii also most likely migrated to Kenya from Uganda, settling near Lake Victoria. But the coming of the Luo in the 1700s, and later aggressive raids by the Kipsigis and the Maasai forced them to move and resettle in the highlands which are still considered to be their homeland.

Despite the raids by the Kipsigis and the Maasai, they were not isolated and got along with the Luo who traded with them. They sold their agricultural products to the Luo and are still some of the best farmers in Kenya.

To the east in the forests of Mount Kenya emerged another culture. The forests of this majestic mountain are also the lands of the Embu and the Chuka.

The Embu are closely related to the Kikuyu and their society is organised on the basis of a close-knit clan system. Their traditional clan system is based on the extended family and all Embu clans belong to one of these groups: *Irumbi* and *Thagana*.

They are great farmers and have taken great advantage of the excellent climate and fertility of the soil to grow a variety of crops and establish a strong, well-structured society in area.

The Chuka seem to be closely related to the Embu but they are considered to be a part of the Meru. And they are all related. The Embu and the Meru are relatives as much as they are relatives of the Kikuyu, also called Gikuyu, and are - together with the Kamba (also known as Akamba) - collectively known as *Gema*, an acronym for Gikuyu, Embu, Meru, and Akamba.

The closest relatives of the Embu are the Mbeere who are also excellent farmers and beekeepers. They are also known for collecting wild honey.

Although fertile and forested regions of Kenya have helped to produce and sustain vibrant cultures and strong communities, arid arid lands have also made their own unique contribution to this development but mainly because of the people who settled there and the different ways they used to cope with and adapt to this harsh environment.

These are mostly the desert regions of northern Kenya including the former Northern Frontier District which is now the North Eastern Province.

Northern Kenya is the cradle of nomadic cultures in the country. And they are mostly Nilotic or Cushitic, contrasted with Bantu cultures in other parts of Kenya and whose people are mostly agriculturalists.

In fact, the remoteness of the region as well as its harsh climate and hostile environment make it one of the world's last frontiers.

It can even be described as an anthropological museum whose cultures and inhabitants together with their beasts of burden range from trips across this arid land by camel caravans of the Rendille tribe to the pride and fighting spirit of the Samburu warriors, their dances and marriage ceremonies.

The Samburu are not well-known like their relatives in the south, the Maasai, but they have a common language and share a complex culture.

An important cultural aspect of where they live – arid or not – is that their culture binds them to these ancestral lands, and the geography or the region itself has reinforced and contributed to the growth of their nomadic culture of which they are very proud and defensive.

Traditionally, Samburu communities were established in areas which provided them with an excellent view of the landscape. This appreciation of nature's beauty and the wilderness is clearly reflected in their own physical appearance which they pay great attention to. They decorate themselves and make sure they look attractive and unique as Samburu.

Even the name Samburu itself is an embodiment of beauty. It means "butterflies"and was given to them by members of another tribe or other tribes, it is said, in acknowledgement of their beauty and the great effort they make to make themselves look good and attractive. Before then, they called themselves Loikop, and still do although the term "Samburu" has gained wider currency.

Rites of passage, or initiation, and warrior culture constitute the back of Samburu society. They are some of the most important aspects of their life as a people which distinguish them from other tribes and give meaning to their temporal existence and even the spiritual dimension of their very being.

Their society is based on age groups defined by a custom called *Olpiroi*, which means "firestick." The "firestick" is handed down, from one age-set to the next, as one generation of *morani* (warriors) becomes responsible for the moral and cultural education of the next. This practice is the foundation not only of the age-hierarchy among the Samburu but also of respect for customs and traditions which hold the community together with its own identity.

Although they differ in some ways in terms of how they live and how they decorate and even see themselves, the Samburu share some customs with their relatives, the Maasai. For example, the blessing of cattle, preparation for war, and victory in a hunt, all of which are celebrated by the Maasai, are also celebrated by the Samburu. And when Samburu warriors dance, they leap high just like the Maasai do, encouraged by the cries of other warriors.

Other similarities between the Samburu and the Maasai include the design and style of the beads they were. The beading is done by women but it is worn by both men and women. But Samburu women don't wear the large flat necklaces Maasai women do. Instead, they wear single loop bead necklaces given to them by their admirers, mostly the *morani*. They are given frequently and soon together form a thick collar.

The Samburu believe that when a girl reaches the age of 15 or 16, she should have enough loops of beads around her neck to support her chin. When she achieves that, she ripe or ready for marriage.

The nomadic life style of the Samburu is one of the most distinctive features of their culture. And they ride camels well-suited to the arid region of northern Kenya. They travel long distances in search of pasture and water for their cows, sheep, and goats.

Tradtionally, they did not have camels. But they acquired them in recent years and got the idea of having these animals probably from the Rendille and the Turkana with whom they have a close relationship and who also live in northern Kenya.

They are so proud of their nomadic life and of being pastoralists that they view farming and any other kind of economic activity that requires settled living as something that is beneath them. And you really don't find farmers in northern Kenya; not the kind you see, for example, in the central highlands or in western Kenya. The north is nomadic country.

Also living in the northern part of Kenya are the Borana, or Boran, who originally came from Ethiopia. In fact, there is still a tribe in Ethiopia with the same name. And Marsabit, located in the central part of northern Kenya, lies at the heart of the ancestral homelands of these people who are very proud of their culture and life style.

Linguistically, the Borana are related to the Galla who include the Oromo. But there is a fundamental difference between the two. The Borana are nomadic; the Galla, agricultural. And the name Borana means "free," in reference to their nomadic life style.

The Borana migrated from Ethiopia to Kenya around 1720 and are therefore relatively new to the region. But during the years they have been there, they have roamed the entire vast expanse in keeping with their nomadic life style.

However, something happened in the 1960s which had a profound impact on their lives. It was a period of major cultural change caused by conflict.

During that period, they had many conflicts with Somali cattle bandits who also roamed the region and the Borana were forced to give up their cattle herds and turn – almost exclusively – to camel husbandry. It was a major and painful change since cattle ownership was, and still is, seen as a symbol of status and a sign of great wealth among most nomads in northern Kenya.

The shift had an even bigger impact on the Borana because cattle ownership was very much an integral part of their cultural identity. This was compounded by the negative attitude the Galla, their relatives, had towards camel ownership.

They considered camels to be lowly and inferior creatures, far beneath cows, and anyone who owned them was equally inferior. This was devastating to the Borana. They went through a fundamental cultural change they never anticipated – until the Somali bandits struck.

The Borana society is basically a structure whose building blocks are family-based clans. Thus, a clan is a collection of related families. The underlying cultural principle of the society is *gada*, an age-set system.

The *gada* principle governs the way a man lives almost his entire life. The first 40 years of a male Borana is divided into five eight-year periods. There are specific beliefs which clearly show what a man may or may not do during each eight-year period, and strict observance of these believes is expected of every man in the Borana society. For example, they show in which eight-year period a man should marry, settle, and have children.

Many Boranas have been converted to Islam and, to a smaller degree, to Christianity. But there are those who still follow traditional religious beliefs. These beliefs are

43

based on reverence for both the supernatural and the natural. Water is seen as a blessing from the heavens, and grass (especially for their livestock, which are camels nowadays) from the earth.

Maintenance of peace within the Borana community is a fundamental principle. The principle is known as *Nagya Borana*, which basically means "Peace of the Boran," and it is the basis of Boran culture. The Boran people believe that all members of the society must at all times be guided by this principle, seek and maintain peace that unites their entire community.

Even when they have conflicts with other tribes, the Boran (or Borana) are always taught to remember that they must maintain peace among themselves. Nothing from outside should be allowed to divide them or cause conflict within the community.

The Boran are closely related to the Gabbra who are also found in many parts of northern Kenya. Like the Boran, they also own camels.

Another tribe of camel owners in this region is the Rendille. But the Rendille are not related to the Boran or the Gabbra. They are, instead, closely related to the Somali who mostly live in northeastern Kenya but from whom they are physically separated by the lands owned by Gabbra-speaking communities.

The Rendille have a reputation as excellent camel herders and handlers and they live as typical nomads, very proud of their nomadic way of life, and very defensive of their life style. They have designed special saddles which enable their camels to carry the entire possessions of a household when families move form one place to another; an achievement - among many others - that enhances their nomadic culture.

An interesting development has taken place between the Rendille and the Samburu through the years. Although the two tribes are not linguistically and genetically related, they have forged strong links between them leading to a

44

strong relationship that has resulted in intermarriage.

One of the most important results of this bond between the two groups has been the evolution of a hybrid culture, in some cases, that has taken place through the years. The culture is neither typical Rendille nor typical Samburu; nor is it entirely alien. But it is unique in its own way as a product of the two.

However, distinct Samburu and Rendille cultures still exist despite the fusion of the two which has taken place in a number of cases. The hybrid culture is not typical of either one.

The focal point of this geographic "wasteland" is Marsabit, a small town whose lush and fertile oasis draws many people of different cultures from all parts of the arid region of northern Kenya.

The intermingling of these people has also led to an intermingling of cultures, making Marsabit some sort of cultural capital or the cosmopolitan centre of northern Kenya. The streets of this small town are a display of different ethnic identities.

There are the Boran, the Rendille, the Samburu, the Gabbra, the Somali, and even the Ethiopians in this region bordering Ethiopia. Add to the mix, tourists from different parts of the world, and even Kenyans of other tribes from the south who now and then visit the north. It is a dazzling array of cultures.

Kenya may not have a lot of natural resources – gold and diamonds, and other minerals – but it is a cultural goldmine.

There is no other country in East Africa (a region composed of Kenya, Uganda and Tanzania) or in the entire region of eastern Africa (that includes the Horn of Africa) which has the kind of ethnic diversity that Kenya has, and on such a large scale.

Kenya's indigenous population is of Bantu stock as well as Nilotic and Cushitic. It is the only country in East Africa which has a very large number of people of

Cushitic origin. Tanzania has Cushitic tribes, especially in the central part of the country, whose members migrated from southern Ethiopia centuries ago. It also has a significant number of Somalis, and a significant number of people of Nilotic origin including the Maasai. But not as much as Kenya does.

The number of people of Nilotic and Cushitic descent in Kenya far surpasses that of Tanzanians of the same origin. Uganda has, if any in significant numbers, even fewer people of Cushitic origin, although it does have large numbers of people of Nilotic descent and more than Tanzania does.

Ethiopia, Somalia, Eritrea and Djibouti don't have any Bantu tribes. They also don't have any Nilotic groups with the possible exception of Ethiopia in the western part of the country bordering Kenya and Sudan, and may be some in the western of Eritrea that also borders Sudan.

It is only Kenya which has all those groups – Bantu, Nilotic and Cushitic – in large numbers as tribes and as part of the total population. And they are native to Kenya although they migrated there from other parts of Africa. But as ethnic groups, they have lived in Kenya long enough to qualify as natives of the country, and legitimately claim the areas where they live as their homelands.

The cultures of all those people have made Kenya unique, not only in East Africa but in the entire region of eastern Africa.

The People of Uganda

THE PEOPLE of Uganda are a diverse mix of ethnic, linguistic and cultural groups.

The vast majority are descended from immigrants who came from the west and the north, waves of migration which formed a confluence in the Great Lakes region, one of the most distinctive parts of Africa.

None of the groups forms a majority of Uganda's population. And the 30 different languages spoken in the country represent an impressive array of ethnic groups and clusters.

Luganda is the most widely spoken local language in the country, especially in the south. It is also the indigenous language of the Buganda kingdom. Other main languages are Lusoga and Runyankore. Lusoga is the main language spoken in Busoga kingdom, and Runyankore or Lunyankole is the main language of Bunyankole.

Swahili is another important language in Uganda and other parts of East and Central Africa. One of its biggest advantages is that it transcends ethnicity and is not identified with any particular tribe or ethnic group, making it acceptable to people of different ethnic and cultural backgrounds.

Its status in Uganda is somewhat controversial. It was approved in 2005 as Uganda's second official language after English. But it has not found wide acceptance across the country. The Bantu groups in the southern and southwestern parts of the country have not accepted Swahili as much as many people in the north have. It is an important lingua franca in the north.

Swahili is also widely used in the police and in the armed forces which had very many northerners during the colonial period and in the first decade of independence.

The language was introduced by the Arabs and other coastal people and was promoted by the colonial authorities to facilitate communication. But it never became widespread in Uganda as it is in Tanzania and to a smaller degree in Kenya. However, efforts have been made by some Ugandan leaders to make it a national language. President Yoweri Museveni has done so, as did Amin.

In terms of demographic composition, three main ethnic groups constitute most of the population in Uganda. They are Bantu, Nilotic, and central-Sudanic traditionally known as Nilo-Hamitic.

The Bantu are the largest. They include the Baganda, the largest ethnic group in Uganda, who live in the central region. Other Bantu groups are the Basoga who live in the southeast; the Banyankole in the southwest; the Bakiga in the most southwestern part of Uganda; the Banyoro in the mid-west; the Batoro or Batooro also in the mid-west; the Bagisu in the east; the Bahima in the southwest; the Bafumbira also in the southwest, and other much smaller ethnic groups.

The Lugbara live mainly in northwestern Uganda and the adjoining area of the Democratic Republic of Congo.

The north is mostly inhabited by the Nilotic who constitute the second-largest group after the Bantu. They include the Iteso who live in the northeast; and the Langi in the central-north.

The other major ethnic group in the north are the Acholi.

The Acholi and the Langi speak almost identical languages. They're also the two largest ethnic groups in northern Uganda.

The most well-known Nilotic group in the northwest is the Lugbara.

The Lugbara live in the highlands on an almost treeless plateau that forms the watershed between the Congo River and the Nile. The Madi live in the lowlands to the east. The two groups speak nearly identical languages and have strong cultural similarities.

Both groups grow millet, cassava, sorghum, legumes, and a variety of root crops. Chicken, goats, and, at higher elevations, cattle are also important. Maize, besides being grown for local consumption, is also used to make beer. Tobacco is an important cash crop.

The Karamojong live in northeastern Uganda. The territory they occupy is considerably drier and largely pastoral.

Ugandans of European, Asian and Arab ancestry constitute 1% of Uganda's population.

There are other smaller groups who are equally an integral part of Uganda.

Baganda

Among all the indigenous groups in the country, probably the Baganda are the most well-known. Their native land, Buganda, was the largest of the former kingdoms in terms of area and constitutes slightly more than one-fourth of Uganda's total land mass.

The family in Buganda is often described as a microcosm of the kingdom. The father is revered and obeyed as head of the family. His decisions are generally unquestioned.

Authoritarian control is a very important part of culture among the Baganda. In precolonial times, obedience to the king was a matter of life and death.

Another very important aspect of culture among the Baganda is emphasis on individual achievement. The Ganda are taught that one's future is not entirely determined by one's status at birth or position in society. Individuals can succeed by working hard and by choosing friends, allies, and patrons carefully. The work ethic is very strong among the Baganda.

In spite of the strong emphasis the Baganda place on ethnic solidarity and cultural pride as well as collective identity, they have not insulated themselves from external influence. And they have historically welcomed outsiders because their culture tolerates diversity.

Even before the coming of Europeans, many Ganda villages included residents from outside Buganda. Some had arrived in the region as slaves and were absorbed and integrated into the society. And since the early 1900s, many non-Baganda migrant workers stayed in Buganda to work on farms.

Also, marriage with non-Baganda was fairly common, and many Baganda marriages ended in divorce. After independence, Ugandan officials estimated that one-third to one-half of all adults marry more than once during their lives.

Traditionally, the economy of the Baganda relied on farming. And even today the majority of the people of Buganda depend on agriculture for their livelihood.

Unlike many other traditional societies in East Africa, cattle ownership played only a minor role in Buganda. Among those who owned cattle, many of them hired labourers from the north as herders.

The most important crop and food commodity was bananas. As a staple food, it sustained the population. It also fuelled population growth.

It also provided a solid foundation for the traditional

economy. And it's still the most important food crop in Buganda even today and plays a major role in the kingdom's economy.

One of the biggest advantages of growing bananas is that the crop does not require shifting cultivation or bush fallowing to maintain soil fertility. That's one of the main reasons why Ganda villages existed as permanent settlements as they still do today.

The Baganda have plenty of food. Besides bananas, they also eat cabbage, beans, peas, mushrooms, carrots, cassava, sweet potatoes, onions, various types of greens, eggs, fish, beans, groundnuts, beef, chicken, and goat meat among other foods. Fruits include pineapples, mangoes, passion fruit, and papaya.

Drinks include indigenous fermented beverages made from bananas (*mwenge*), pineapples (*munanansi*), and maize (*musoli*).

The Baganda have very fertile land. Most of them are peasants who live in rural villages. Rich red clay on hillsides, a moderate temperature, and plentiful rainfall combine to provide a good environment for the year-round availability of bananas as well as the seasonal production of coffee, cotton, and tea as cash crops.

The Baganda are also well-known for their basketry, especially mat-making by women. The mats are colourful and intricately designed.

In Ganda society – or the Buganda kingdom – men traditionally cleared the fields and tilled the land while women planted crops. Men also engaged in commerce. There was a clear division of labour in many areas of life but those distinctions are now blurred in the modern economy.

However, differences remain in a number of areas. There are still many tasks which men or women are not supposed to do.

There are also many important economic activities which are no longer the exclusive domain of men. Some people, especially traditionalists, decry the change. Others, especially women and those of the younger generations, welcome it.

Some of the major changes which have taken place in the traditional society as a result of Westernisation include adoption of Christianity. It has transformed the traditional way of life so much that religious beliefs of the ancestors no longer play the kind of role they once did.

And the contrast is glaring. In the second half of the 1800s, most Baganda were practising an indigenous form of religion known as *Balubaale*.

It consisted of gods who had temples identified with them. The gods were each concerned with specific problems. For example, there was a god of fertility, a god of warfare, and a god of the lake.

The Baganda also believed in spiritual forces, particularly the action of witches, which were thought to cause illness and other misfortunes. People often wore amulets (charms) to ward off their evil powers.

The most significant spirits were the *muzimu* or ancestors who visited the living in dreams and sometimes warned of impending dangers.

But *Balubaale* is no longer practised by many people in Buganda. However, belief in the power of the departed ancestors and in witchcraft is still prevalent. It probably will never die.

Banyoro

Another kingdom, Bunyoro, which played a major role in the establishment, evolution and growth of Buganda, had its own history of achievements which included the development of complex cultural and political institutions whose influence spread far beyond its borders.

Other political entities such as the princedom of Busoga, besides Buganda kingdom, also benefited from the achievements of Bunyoro. Their own institutions, at least some of them, were a byproduct of Bunyoro since some of these societies were partly established by the people who migrated from Bunyoro or were heavily influenced by Bunyoro.

The history of Bunyoro is a history of some of the greatest achievements – in terms of cultural, political, social and institutional development – in the history of precolonial Africa.

From the 16th to the 19th century, Bunyoro was the most powerful kingdom in the area that later came to be known as Uganda; it was also one of the most powerful in the entire East Africa. Even today, its traditional ruler, the Omukama, remains an important figure in Ugandan politics, especially among the Banyoro people of whom he is the titular head.

Located in western Uganda in the area east of Lake Albert, the kingdom of Bunyoro even today has strong traditional ties to Toro which was once part of Bunyoro. And the Bunyoro language is also spoken in Toro.

The Banyoro are Bantu. But their kingdom was founded by Nilotic people from the north.

Every Munyoro (singular) belongs to a clan which is a group of people who are descended from the same ancestor. They're therefore blood relatives.

The Banyoro are predominantly agricultural. But they also own cattle which play an important role in their lives. And while the kingdom's economy is heavily dependent on agricultural commodities as is the case in most parts of Uganda, the discovery of oil in the kingdom is expected to transform this traditional society in significant ways.

The demand for a significant share of oil revenues by the Bunyoro kingdom is also inextricably linked with the kingdom's demand for greater autonomy – now enjoyed by all the kingdoms but only in the cultural sphere – and assertion of its identity as a cultural and political entity in the context of Uganda.

It's a demand that has been shared by other kingdoms in Uganda through the years since independence and found its most forceful expression among the Baganda in the mid-sixties when they wanted to secede and establish their own independent state.

The Banyoro may not have gone as far as the Baganda did in the mid-sixties, demanding full independence if their aspirations could not be realised in a federal context. But they have demanded nothing less in terms of autonomy. And they attribute many of the problems they face to the abolition of kingdoms by President Milton Obote in 1967.

There is an imperative need for traditional entities to have autonomy in a number of areas in order to maintain their identities and pursue goals in their own political and social contexts in countries where the national government does not allow the people at the grassroots level to be active participants in the political process and find solutions to their own problems.

It also goes to the heart of what constitutes Uganda as a single political entity. And it raises fundamental questions about the nature of relations between the country's various ethnic groups and even challenges the protocols of association the nation's different ethnic entities have with the central government in the context of a modern African state.

While Uganda remains a unitary state, to the consternation of many people who would like to see a federal structure instituted, the authorities at the centre should admit that there is a need for decentralisation to enable the people to realise their aspirations across the spectrum at the local and regional levels.

Decentralisation also defuses tensions between the central government and the regions and helps to maintain peace and stability. It also strengthens national unity and neutralises secessionist tendencies.

Unity in diversity is one of the fundamental principles

which must be upheld by the members of hetereogenous societies who want to achieve prosperity, peace and stability for all. All that is impossible without an equitable distribution of wealth.

Others also demand their share of the national cake. They include the kingdoms of Toro and Ankole and the princedom of Busoga which together with Bunyoro and Buganda have earned Uganda distinction as the most "aristocratic" nation in East Africa.

But the Banyoro feel that they have a special claim to the wealth generated by oil found in their territory. And it has potential for disaster.

If the oil wealth is not distributed well, Uganda could have a situation similar to what has happened in the Niger Delta in Nigeria where the indigenous people have not benefited from the sale of oil pumped from under their feet.

Since the early 1950s when oil was discovered in Nigeria, the country has earned more than $600 billion. Yet the people of Nigeria are still some of the poorest in the world, and the indigenes in the Niger Delta some of the most exploited. They have nothing to show for all that wealth earned from their soil except polluted land and water including fish, endangering the lives of millions of people in the region.

There's no guarantee Uganda will avoid all that even if the situation does not become as extreme as it is in Nigeria.

In all the African countries where oil has been found, it has been both a curse and a blessing.

In fact, in most cases oil wealth has been more of a curse than a blessing. Uganda is no exception. Bunyoro may become the Niger Delta of the Great Lakes region, if not of the entire East Africa.

Even neighbouring Tanzania with its substantial mineral wealth hardly gets anything from its newly-found wealth. Most of it goes to foreigners who work in collusion with many government officials to exploit the people.

Batoro

Right next to Bunyoro in the south is the kingdom of Toro which once was an integral part of the large empire of Kitara. The empire included areas of present day central, western, and southern Uganda; northern Tanzania, western Kenya, and eastern Congo. The Bachwezi are credited with the founding of the Kitara empire.

In addition to founding the empire of Kitara, the Bachwezi are further credited with the introduction of the unique, long-horned Ankole cattle, coffee growing, iron smelting, and the first semblance of organised and centralised government, under the king.

No one knows what happened to the Bachwezi. There is a popular belief among scholars that they simply got assimilated into the indigenous populace and are, today, the tribal groups like the Bahima of Ankole and the Batutsi of Rwanda.

Usually, the Bahima and the Batutsi are tall and have a light complexion. It's said that the Bachwezi also looked that way. They're also herders of the long-horned Ankole cattle just as the Bachwezi were. And the blood of the Bachwezi still runs through the veins of many people in the kindoms of southwestern Uganda including Toro.

Like other Africans in most traditional societies, the Toro are conservative in general but probably more conservative than many other people in Uganda. For example, old taboos which have been observed for centuries are still observed today even when they're counterproductive.

Modernisation has had an impact on Toro society, sometimes in a profound way, but not enough to change the traditional way of life in all its aspects.

The Toro are also known for their traditional dances. They have two main ones. One is called *ntogoroo* and the other one is known as *amatimbo*.

Their traditional foods of the Toro are millet, sorghum, sweet potatoes, bananas, peas, beans, groundnuts, green vegetables including cabbage, and firinda.

Milk and butter are also part of their diet. The cattle-owing Bahima provide milk and butter, while the agriculturalist Bairu grow food crops.

In spite of the abundance of fish in the lakes of Toro, fish has never been an integral part of the Toro diet because of cultural taboos.

Although it is small, the Toro kingdom stands out as one of the most prominent traditional societies in Uganda and in the entire East Africa.

Banyankole

Another major kingdom is Ankole, one of the big four in the Great Lakes area of what later came to be known as Uganda.

While the identity of Toro is inextricably linked with that of Bunyoro, the former being a product of the latter, that of Ankole stands on its own in a number of ways. But Ankole was also heavily influenced by Bunyoro, as were the rest of the kingdoms, since Bunyoro was the most powerful in the Greal Lakes region for centuries.

The people of Ankole are called Banyankole or Banyankore; in singular form it's Munyankole or Munyankore. The Ankole kingdom is also known as Nkore.

It was traditionally ruled by a monarch known as *mugabe* or *omugabe* of Ankole, a title equivalent to that of *kabaka* in the Buganda kingdom and *omukama* in Bunyoro.

The establishment of the Ankole kingdom is attributed

to the Hima, also known known as Bahima. They became a dominant force in the Great Lakes region until they were replaced by the colonial rulers as the dominant power.

The Banyakole are also well-known for their cows known as Ankole. In fact, one of the most famous breeds of cows in East Africa is Ankole. Ankole cows are known for their long horns.

But there are also fears that it may be a dying breed. They have been an integral part of life in the Great Lakes region for centuries. But that may no longer be the case after a few decades.

Even when the Ankole cow is no more, if the breed will indeed be gone one day, the people in the Great Lakes region who have relied on this domesticated animal for centuries will continue to live the same way.

They're still going to have cows, only of a different breed or breeds.

And the people of the Ankole kingdom, well-known as cow owners and as farmers, will always be among those who will benefit the most from the new breed or breeds of cows as they continue to live their traditional way of life but only with different results.

The cows they're going to have are going to be more productive, giving them more milk, hence more economic security and better health.

But it will also be tragic. The old ways, of owning the Ankole cows and all that it entails in a cultural context including its spiritual dimension since this breed of cows has been an integral of life in the Great Lakes region for centuries, will be lost forever.

Just like other Africans, the Ankole are a proud people. They're proud of their culture and traditional way of life. And they don't want to lose it. They're also proud of their ethnic identity as Ankole different from other ethnic groups.

And theirs is "the land where milk and honey freely flow down the village paths."

But they also have differences among themselves.

Yet the people of Ankole are united as a single cultural entity whose ethnic bonds transcend political differences. Traditionalists and modernists, even ethnic chauvinists and nationalists who want one Uganda as a single nation, are all inextricably linked, constituting one of the most well-known ethnic groups in Uganda and in the whole of East Africa.

Like other Ugandans, they are a people with their own traditional homeland, their own customs and way of life handed down through the generations. And they cherish the memory of their history and keep alive the traditions of their ancestors just as other Ugandans do.

Although Uganda is a product of a few old kingdoms and many smaller independent chieftaincies, its traditional landscape – in terms of prominence and importance – is dominated by only a few traditional institutions.

The communities which have been organised in traditional institutions of kingdoms – and princedoms – are the Baganda under the *kabaka*, the Banyoro under the *omukama*, the Banyankole under the *omugabe*, the Batoro also under the *omukama* like the Banyoro, the Basoga under the k*yabazinga*, the Alur under the *rwoth-obima*, the Ateso under the e*morimori*, and the Bakonjo under the *omumbere*.

The kingdom of Ankole reached a level of sophistication during pre-colonial times which even impressed European explorers. They were amazed at the sophisticated and cultured societies they found not only in Ankole but in neighbouring kingdoms.

The kingdom of Ankole in southwestern Uganda was known not only for its long-horned cattle – as it still is – but also its absolute ruler, *mugabe* (king) who claimed that all the cattle in the land belonged to him. And the chiefs under him were ranked on the basis of how many cattle they had.

It was also a society divided on the basis of social

classes. It was a kind of caste system although not as rigid as the one in India. The cattle owners, the Bahima, belonged to the higher class, and the Bairu farmers to the lower class.

And the country was excellent for livestock, with its rolling plains covered with abundant grass. But grazing land has diminished through the years because of high population growth.

The Banyankole are also known to be good story tellers. Riddles and proverbs are also very important in conversations and as a means to impart wisdom and teach the young their proper role in society. Combined with tales and legends, they also teach proper moral behaviour to the young. Of special significance are legends surrounding the institution of the kingship, which provide a historical framework for the Banyankole.

Although Christianity is prevalent, many Banyankole – including a significant number of Christians – pay a lot of attention to traditional secular and religious practices. The belief in ancestor spirits is very strong. Many Banyankole believe that if you neglect a dead realative, you incur the wrath of the ancestors. And an offering such as meat or milk must be offered to appease them.

In many respects, little has changed since the good old days especially in terms of customs and traditions mainly in the rural areas.

Like all other Africans in pre-colonial times, the Banyankole were an independent people. They had their own institutions and their own rulers.

Among the Banyankole, the quest for the restoration of the Ankole kingdom is not only fuelled by nostalgia for the past but also by contemporary necessities in the political and economic realms.

It's the only former kingdom which has not regained its former status. But it may also be the only kingdom in Uganda where a significant number of people don't want to reinstitute the monarchy while at the same time retaining pride in their political and cultural achievements and ethnic identity.

The demand for the restoration of the kingdom is supported even by some of the most ardent Ugandan nationalists among the Banyankole who are committed to maintaining the territorial integrity of Uganda as a single nation. They don't see any contradiction between the two. And they are committed to achieving both.

The debate over the status of the kingdoms is a divisive issue among many Ugandans in different parts of the country. And it may not end until all the kingdoms regain their former status even if with diminished influence in terms of political power.

And they all have been accorded that status except Ankole, even though there are still some demands from all the kingdoms which have not been met by the government.

Full restoration of political power, and the establishment of a federal form of government with extensive devolution of power to the kingdoms and the regions, are the biggest demands which have not yet been met. And they probably never will in the context of modern Uganda.

But that has not stifled nationalist aspirations at the micro-national level in the kingdoms which in many ways still see themselves as nations, as they indeed once were during pre-colonial times, regardless of how anachronistic they may be in the context of the modern African state which eschews and transcends ethnicity.

And among all the kingdoms, the most vocal demands come from Ankole because it has not been allowed to regain its former status as a traditional kingdom.

Many Banyankole may have accepted fate and probably believe that their glorious past can not be reclaimed and relived in the form of a restored kingdom. But there are still many others who believe that there are better days ahead.

They look to the future of a reinvigorated past, a golden era of cultural revival and pride even if they may never again enjoy the political power they once had during the good old days before the advent of imperial rule.

Basoga

Another well-known traditional political and cultural grouping in Uganda is the princedom of Busoga. It is also one of the most prominent ethnic entities in the Great Lakes region of East Africa.

Its people, the Basoga, are organised on the basis of clans, a common feature in many traditional societies across the continent. They're also closely related to the Baganda and the Banyoro as well other Bantu ethnic groups in Uganda and across the border in Kenya.

Most of the people are farmers. The vast majority of them grow crops on small farms for their own consumption.

The main commercial crops are sugarcane and tea. They are grown on plantations.

Other crops include bananas, maize, millet, rice, sweet potatoes, fruits and vegetables.

The northern part of Busoga is known for its cattle and other domesticated animals including sheep and goats. It also supports agriculture. But the region, especially Kamuli District, is known for its cattle more than anything else and is a part of the cattle corridor of East Africa.

The people of Busoga are known as Basoga – singular Musoga. And they speak Lusoga, a Bantu language. It evolved from a combination of several dialects to become one of the most prominent local languages in Uganda. It's related to Lunyoro and Luganda.

The origin of the Basoga also is inextricably linked with the origin of other Bantu groups who trace their roots to what's now Congo and before then West Africa, especially what's now Cameroon and eastern Nigeria.

It's believed that the earliest inhabitants of the region that's now Busoga were the Langi who today are – together with the Acholi – one of the main ethnic groups in northern Uganda. The Iteso and the Bagishu or Bagisu also preceded the Basoga in what's now Busoga. And the Basoga were later overwhelmed by the Baganda.

Besides the Baganda and the Banyoro as the founders of the Busoga kingdom (princedom), there was another major Bantu group which played a role in the establishment of this traditional entity. They were the Banyankole. They're are said to be some of the earliest settlers in Busoga who occupied the shore areas near Lake Victoria and were later joined by other people from the Mount Elgon area.

Other people from different parts of what's now western Kenya also migrated into the area during those early years.

The impact of all these outside influences has been profound on the evolution of Busoga in terms of ethnic composition, linguistic development, and cultural fusion.

Although Busoga was not as strong as Bunyoro or Buganda in terms of political power and military might, it was the most integrated traditional "kingdom" in terms of ethnic composition when the colonial rulers arrived.

It was a product of many ethnic groups and cultures. And its existence as an integrated society is strong testimony to the political genius of its founders and its people who have worked together through the decades to create one of the most cohesive traditional societies on the African continent.

The traditional homeland of the Basoga also has many tourist attractions. Their capital, Jinja, is not only one of the most important towns in Uganda and in the entire East Africa; it's also the source of the Nile.

It's at Jinja where River Nile starts to flow north out of Lake Victoria. And many people from many parts of the world visit Jinja every year to see the source of the Nile.

But that's just one of the major attractions Busoga has. Its strategic location alone on the shores of Lake Victoria is enough to draw countless visitors every year and is a major asset to Uganda.

Bakiga

Other major Bantu groups in Uganda – besides the Baganda, Banyoro, Batoro and Basoga – include the Bakiga and the Bagisu.

The Bakiga live mostly in Kabale District – which once was a part of the larger Kigezi District before it was split up – in southwestern Uganda. They straddle the Ugandan-Rwandan border and also live in northwestern Rwanda. They're sometimes called northern Hutus.

They migrated to Uganda from what's now Rwanda between 1600s and 1700s.

They have also migrated to other parts of Uganda because of overpopulation in their homeland in the southwestern part of the country.

And this has led to conflict with other ethnic groups including their neighbours such as the Banyoro and those much farther away such as the Baganda. Some of the conflicts have been over land ownership.

The inter-tribal or inter-ethnic conflicts over land raises serious questions about national unity and identity. Do members of different ethnic groups see themselves as fellow Ugandans first, or does their ethnic identity take precedence over national identity?

It seems the majority of them consider themselves Banyoro, Bakiga, or Baganda; so do the rest. Their tribe comes first. That's also the case in Kenya, Rwanda and Burundi. Tanzania is the only exception among the East African countries where tribalism has virtually been conquered.

The tribal conflicts over land – and over anything else – are symptomatic of a much deeper problem: the inability and unwillingness to transcend tribal loyalties and rivalries for the sake of national unity. Many people simply refuse to accept each other as equals and as fellow citizens in spite of their common identity as Ugandans.

The politics of ethnicity even acquired the stamp of "legitimacy" when a few years earlier some members of parliament also blamed the Bakiga for "grabbing" land which belonged to the Baganda and other ethnic groups.

Such ethnophobia has a tendency to spread and feed on itself. And it's highly contagious. It could destroy the social fabric of Uganda which holds the people together as a single nation with equal rights including the right to live wherever they want to live.

The Bakiga are only one group who have incurred the wrath of their fellow countrymen for moving into areas where they are not welcome and where they are seen as foreigners in their own country.

The Bakiga speak Rukiga, a Bantu language. And they share cultural traits – perhaps even biological ties – with the Banyambo of northwestern Tanzania. One theory even suggests that they migrated from Karagwe in what's now northwestern Tanzania. But historical evidence shows that the Bakiga who settled in southwestern Uganda came from northwestern neighbouring Rwanda.

Their social organisation is based on clans like that of many other African ethnic groups.

Traditionally, the Bakiga are a very polygamous society. The number of wives is only limited by the availability of land and bride wealth obligations. That was especially the case in the past when polygamy was even more widespread. But it's an institution that's cherished even today as much as it is in many traditional societies across Africa.

Traditional religion is still strong among the Bakiga although many of them have been converted to

65

Christianity. There are only a few Muslims.

But even some Christians uphold traditional beliefs and subscribe to the tenets of ancestor "worship" – reverence for their wisdom and guidance from the world beyond and for the role they play in interceding with the Almighty on behalf of the living.

The Bakiga traditionally believe in the existence of a Supreme Being whom they call Ruhanga as the Creator of all things earthly and heavenly; a concept no different from Christianity and which pre-dates the introduction of Christianity to the Bakiga by European missionaries.

But for centuries, they also believed in the cult of Nyabingi. Sacrifices and offerings – including roasted meat and beer – were made to Nyabingi, the spirit of a much-respected rain maker. And they're still made by some people even today because of their strong belief in traditional religion.

The economy of the Bakiga is based on agriculture. They grow mainly sorghum, millet, beans and peas. They also own cows, sheep and goats.

They traditionally also have had excellent iron-smiths making hoes, knives, spears and other implements. They also make excellent pottery, baskets, mats, furniture items and others. They're also very good bee keepers and collect honey.

The Bakiga are some of the most tradition-bound people in the Great lakes region. And they're deeply rooted in their homeland which is a mountainous area. In fact, the name of their ethnic group, Abakiga (shortened to Bakiga), means "people of the mountains" or "highlanders."

Bagisu

On the other side of Uganda are another Bantu group, the Bagisu, one of the most well-known ethnic groups in the country and in the Great Lakes region.

The Bagisu live mainly in Mbale District on the slopes of Mount Elgon in eastern Uganda. They're a sub-group of the Bamasaaba people of eastern Uganda and are closely related to the Bukusu which is a sub-group the Luhya of Kenya.

The term Bamasaaba is used interchangeably with the term Bagisu, now and then, in spite of the fact that they're different. The Bagisu are Bamasaaba but not all Bamasaaba are Bagisu.

They speak a dialect of the Masaaba language called Lugisu which is not much different from the other dialects within the Bamasaaba group of languages. Lugisu is also understood by the Bukusu.

All the Masaaba understand each other even when they speak different dialects of the Masaaba language. And Lugisu is also called Lumasaaba. The Bagisu themselves are also known as Bamasaaba.

The Bagisu mainly inhabit the western and southern halves Mountain Elgon. The eastern part of Mount Elgon is in Kenya.

They grow millet, bananas an maize on the well-watered slopes of the mountain mainly for their own consumption. They also grow coffee and cotton as cash crops.

Other crops they grow include sweet and white potatoes, cabbage and other vegetables as well as onions and tomatoes. They also own cattle and other livestock.

Bugisu, their homeland, has the highest population density in Uganda. Almost all land is used for growing crops. Shortage of land has forced many people to leave their traditional homeland and settle elsewhere in Uganda. It also has led to social conflicts now and then through the years.

The Bagisu were introduced to cash crop farming on a significant scale when arabica coffee was brought to them in 1912. The expansion of British colonial rule into Bugisu also played a major role in introducing the Bagisu to a cash economy.

And the people became very successful in the production of cash crops. The climate was highly conducive to farming and the Bagisu were able to produce large amounts of coffee. They also used this as a bargaining tool with the colonial government to extract concessions favourable to them by threatening to withhold production until their demands were met.

The farmers formed the Bugisu Cooperative Union to protect the interests of coffee growers and it became one of the most powerful and most active agricultural cooperative unions in the entire country.

Their economic clout became even more potent because the coffee they grew on the fertile slopes of Mount Elgon was of the highest quality in Uganda. And the total output from that small region constituted more than 10 per cent of the nation's total production.

This provided the Bagisu with a very effective bargaining tool, enabling them to have leverage in their negotiations with the authorities for higher prices for their crops and on other matters pertaining to their interests and well-being.

Land pressure during the early decades of colonial rule forced the Bagisu to migrate northwards, a migratory trend which brought them into conflict with the Sebei who have fought against Gisu dominance for over a century. They saw the Bagisu as invaders encroaching on their territory. And they were not alone in taking that position. Other people felt the same way.

Members of other ethnic groups, the Bagwere and the Bakedi in areas south of Bugisu have also claimed distinct cultural identities and have sought political autonomy.

The Bagisu have no tradition of an early migration from somewhere. And very little is known about their history apart from the fact they're related to a sub-group of the Luhya.

The Luhya are the second largest ethnic in Kenya next

to the Kikuyu after surpassing the Luo who once were the second-largest. And because their history is known, it must be inextricably linked with the history of the Bagisu in some ways since the Bukusu who are an integral part of the Luo are related to the Bagisu.

Although not much of their history is known, the Bagisu are believed to have separated from the Bukusu sometime during the 1800s, despite their claim that they have lived where they are all the time; no people have. We all came from somewhere.

The earliest immigrants into Bugisu area are believed to have moved into the Mt. Elgon area during the 16th century from the eastern plains.

Their earliest home is said to have been in the Uasin Gishu plateau of Kenya.

They seem to have been an end product of the mixing of peoples of different origins and cultures, but since their language is Bantu, their predecessors must have been Bantu speakers as well.

Traditionally, the Bagisu had a loose political structure based on clans. Every clan had an elder known as *Umwami we sikoka* which means chief of the clan.

The Bagisu practise male circumcision although they don't know how and when it became an integral part of their culture. They may have learnt it from the Kalenjin of Kenya.

The men are not considered to be fully grown or mature unless they're circumcised. They take it so seriously that some people are forcibly circumcised.

Even many of those who undergo circumcision have been converted to Christianity and don't necessarily follow traditional religion. But traditional beliefs including customs such as circumcision are deeply rooted among the Bagisu in general despite widespread influences of modernisation and Western civilisation which have had quite an impact on the traditional way of life.

Many Bagisus, probably the majority, are Christian.

There are also some Muslims. But traditional religion is still strong even among a significant number of those who are Christian.

One of the most prominent features which distinguishes traditional African societies is adherence to customs and traditions. The Bagisu are a typical example of that.

Circumcision as a rite of passage is just one of those practices in a panoply of customs and traditions which define many traditional societies in Uganda and other parts of Africa.

Although the Bagisu are Bantu and practise cicumcision, the practice is not as widespread among the Bantu as it is among Nilotics. Almost all Nilotic groups such as the Karamojong, the Kalenjin, the Maasai and others practise circumcision.

But in societies where it's practised, even those who may be against it succumb to the knife because there's so much social pressure exerted on them. Failure to do so leads to ostracisation.

Not only do they become social outcasts; they're not considered manly and may not even be able to marry, something which is frowned upon in most traditional societies across Africa.

Among Bantu groups which don't traditionally practise circumcision, the only people who must be circumcised are Muslims since that's mandatory according to Islam.

But it's also a very painful experience. Some people who have come under the knife have written about their ordeal, as did, for example, Nelson Mandela, a Xhosa, in his book *Long Walk to Freedom*.

The Xhosa, the second-largest ethnic group in South Africa after the Zulu, are among the Bantu groups which practise circumcision.

Among the Bagisu, there's also acceptance of both – the pain and the necessity to be circumcised – and also of the pride in their culture which holds the people together

70

as a group with their own unique identity and way of life. It's a wonderful journey into manhood, however painful.

Lugbara

Another ethnic group that's examined in this study is the Lugbara of northwestern Uganda.

They're one of the largest Nilotic groups in the country. They live mainly in the West Nile region of Uganda and in the adjoining area of the Democratic Republic of Congo (DRC).

Their language, Lugbara, has many dialects. But the people who speak those dialects understand each other. In addition to the Madi, the Lugbara are also related to the Kakwa and understand each other when they speak their languages.

They're also closely related to the Logo, 'Bale (Lendu), and Keliko, and are distantly related to the Azande and the Mangbetu.

They and the Madi, their neighbours to the east, are the only representatives of the eastern Sudanic language group in eastern Africa.

Their cultural symbol is the leopard. And they're very conscious of their singular identity geographically, linguistically, and culturally. Their plateau is very distinct from the landscapes of most of their neighbours.

They're farmers and also own livestock, mainly cattle and goats. They also have sheep.

Before the cattle epidemics of the 1980s, they had far greater herds. Cattle, goats, and sheep are also killed for ancestral sacrifices and meat is consumed by those attending the ceremonies. The Lugbara also sell hides and skins, earning valuable income.

They also own poultry and are known in Uganda as the main keepers of the guineafowl which is known as *ope* in their language.

There's also a sharp division of labour between men and women. Men clear the fields while the women do the rest of the work. Men also hunt and herd cattle while women do domestic work.

The Lugbara irrigate their farms. And some of their fields are also under permanent or shifting cultivation..

Traditionally, their social organisation was based on clans and sub-clans. Chiefdoms came later, introduced by the colonial rulers who appointed locally influential men as chiefs. Below the chefs were headmen The Lugbara never had a king or paramount ruler.

The chiefs usually formed alliances to ensure security and mobilise forces against attacks by other ethnic groups. But they did not have a standing army.

Every able-bodied man was duty-bound to protect his village. Therefore all men were automatically considered to be soldiers ready to answer the call whenever needed. However, military service was never considered to be a permanent duty.

Men hold formal authority over their kin but older women informally exercise considerable domestic and lineage authority. Land is traditionally not sold or rented; it's held by lineages. Women are also allocated rights of use by their husbands' lineage elders.

Marriage is forbidden between members of the same clan or with a man's or woman's mother's close kin. And polygamy is widespread. About a third of the men have more than one wife. However, most secondary wives are those inherited from their brothers or fathers' brothers. A number of other African tribes have the same custom of inheriting wives from dead brothers.

Some even inherit wives of their dead fathers in a number of traditional societies on the continent. Their step mothers become their wives, although this is not practised by the Lugbara.

Divorce is relatively unusual among the Lugbara. And only men can seek divorce. The parents or relatives of the divorced woman or women are required to return cattle given to them as dowry. But if there are children involved, a different formula is used. For every child born, a cow is kept, not returned.

The main grounds for divorce are adultery and barrenness. In fact, in many traditional societies in Africa, a man can ask for divorce if a woman can not bear children.

There are no forms of initiation at puberty, but children of about 6 undergo forehead cicatrization and excision of the lower four incisors.

The Lugbara country is open, composed of countless small ridges with streams between them. The compounds and fields are set on the ridges. Houses are round. They're made of mud and wattle and thatch.

If a man has more than one wife, he moves from one house to another in turn. The house, and especially its hearth, is very much a female domain.

Traditional religion has played a prominent in the lives of the Lugbara. And it continues to do so.

Even before the coming of Europeans who introduced Christianity, the Lugbra believed in a single deity called *Adroa*. They believed, as they still do today, that He created the world and everything in it.

They also believe that there's a world of spirits and departed ancestors. The spirits influence the affairs of men, as do departed ancestors, and sacrifices must be offered to appease them.

The Lugbara believe that the living interact with the dead of the same lineage and that this relationship is permanent. Because of this close relationship, the dead know what's going on among the living whom they still consider to be their children.

However, in some circumstances, the dead send sickness to the living, in order to remind them that they are acting custodians of the Lugbara lineages and their shrines.

Also, there have been prophets among the Lugbara during hard times and periods of crisis. Divinely-inspired messages, according to those who believe this, have involved the reorganisation of the social order, among other things.

The most famous prophet among the Lugbara was Rembe who led an anti-European healing cult in 1916. He was actually a member of the Kakwa tribe and lived about 40 miles north of Lugbara.

But many of them have also embraced Christianity and are mostly Catholic.

There are also a few Muslims in the region, especially in the few small townships. These are usually Nubians – also called Nubi – and they are not typical Lugbara.

The most prominent Muslim from the West Nile region was Idi Amin who came from the neighbouring Kakwa tribe.

Although the Lugbara are engaged in agriculture, they're not commercial farmers.

Cash crops were encouraged during the colonial period, but, owing to edaphic and climatic factors and the long distance to the nearest markets for cash crops, few have been profitable.

The best markets are in the southern part of the country where the capital Kampala is also located. That's hundreds of miles away, discouraging many people in the West Nile from engaging in commercial agriculture.

Groundnuts, sunflower, cotton, and tobacco have all been tried as commercial crops. But only the latter two, cotton and tobacco, have had some success.

The main export has been that of male labour to the Indian-owned sugar plantations and the African-owned farms of southern Uganda. About one-quarter of the men are absent at any one time, making the Lugbara some of the most well-known migrant workers in Uganda.

Almost all farming is restricted to the subsistence level. They grow a variety of crops but cassava is now their staple food. Traditionally, they have relied on millet and sorghum.

Besides millet and sorghum, they also grow pigeon peas and a variety of root crops including sweet potatoes. But with their increasing dependency on cassava, their diet has deteriorated. Traditionally, they had a highly nutritious diet.

They also grow maize for local consumption and for making local beer. Their main cash crop is tobacco.

Their land is very fertile. They are also known to be very good farmers even though they grow crops on a small scale mainly for their own consumption.

They are, in general tall people, taller than the average Ugandan, and are skillful hunters using mainly bows and long arrows.

They're also known for making very good baskets and pots. Besides pottery and basketry, they have few other aesthetic products. They don't make elaborate carvings or skillfully handle metal.

The iron-smiths among them are members of an ethnic group called Ndu. These skilled workers make iron tools and weapons. They live scattered among the Lugbara settlements and are held in awe by them. They're also feared by the Lugbara as if they have some mystical powers because of their iron-working skills.

But the Lugbara also have a reputation as fierce fighters and are very defensive of their land. It was this ability to fight and defend themselves which saved them from being enslaved by the marauding Arab slave traders who were active to the north and west during the 19th century.

Although many of them have been converted to Christianity, modernisation has not penetrated their society as much as it has other parts of Uganda especially in the southern kingdoms. Theirs is a much more traditional way of life, and conservative.

Batwa

The Batwa, or Twa, live in southwestern Uganda. They're also known as Pygmies.

They're also found across the border in neighbouring Congo and Rwanda.

They live in the forest and have a strong attachment to their homeland. They believe that when God made them, He wanted them to live in the forest and protect it.

They also like to be close to nature in an environment where it's quiet and peaceful. And they may the original people together with the so-called Bushmen.

They have lived in the forest for a long time. This has enabled them to develop survival skills unmatched by members of other ethnic groups who may try to live in this kind of environment.

The forest provides them with herbs for medicine. They use traditional medicine for all kinds of ailments and don't depend on modern medicine for treatment.

They're also excellent hunters. They use bows and arrows, spears and machetes as well as knives. Their reputation as excellent users of bows and arrows is legendary. They also use the same weapons to defend themselves.

One of the biggest items in their diet is honey which is also excellent for fighting diseases. And besides meat, wild fruit as well as vegetables and mushrooms are an integral part of their diet.

They have been mostly hunter-gatherers, some in the mountainous forests, and some in forest savannah or lake environments.

They're despised by their neighbours but maintain their dignity by living in isolation.

Many of their neighbours don't even see them as human.

Their neighbours are mostly Bantu except the Tutsi.

They're also known as forest people who live in the rain-forests of east-central Africa and as far afield as Cameroon and the Central African Republic.

Other countries in which they live are the Democratic Republic of Congo, Rwanda, Burundi, Congo-Brazzaville and Gabon.

But their means of livelihood have been severely affected through the years, reducing them to desperate conditions in some parts of the east-central and west-central regions of Africa.

In all those countries, they suffer discrimination, only in varying degrees. And their plight can be better understood when look at in a larger context embracing all these groups of marginalised people in that part of the continent.

Many Batwas in southwestern Uganda have been forced by the government to move out of the forest, disrupting their traditional way of life and causing extreme hardship for them. They have lost their homes and means of livelihood without getting any help from the government.

In 1991, the Bwindi and Mgahinga National Parks were established in southwestern Uganda, causing great suffering to Batwa and other neighbouring local communities.

The Batwa are by far the most affected group since they no longer have access to their forest resources, and so their forest-based participation in the local economy has been destroyed. They have been reduced to being landless labourers. They are also victimised by other groups who discriminate against them.

But they're survivors. They have lived in the forest for thousands of years. They know how to fend for themselves. Their skills have ensured their survival. But there are those who fear the Batwa may be extinct one day.

While some observers don't go to that extreme, saying the Batwa face extinction, many of them are equally apprehensive of the situation and concede that if nothing is done to protect them, they face a bleak future.

The Ugandan government and others in the region – as well as the ones in southern Africa especially Botswana where another marginalised people, the San and the Khoi live – are pursuing a policy of modernisation to force these people to abandon their traditional way of life and become part of the modern society.

But such a policy is bound to fail because the people who are being forced to change don't want to change. Even for those who want to do so, more often than not, only grudgingly, it's obvious that they can not change right away because adaptation can not be done overnight.

Tragically, in this clash of civilisations or cultures, the marginalised groups end up being the losers. It's also a form of cultural genocide.

And their future is indeed bleak. According to a report by Thomas Fessy, BBC World Service, "Batwa Face Uncertain Future":

"Just after dawn, as the fog slowly leaves the slopes of the Muhabura volcano, some Batwa people make their way to the neighbouring farms hoping to get a job for the day.

The Nyarusisa community is landless. Families are squatting on other people's land or live in shabby camps with no sanitation.

The Muhabura volcano is one of the three inactive volcanoes that make the south-west Ugandan border with Rwanda and the Democratic Republic of Congo.

Right next to the Mgahinga National Park's boundaries, the slopes of these mountains are intensively cultivated and settled by dominant Bufumbira and Hutu people.

Nearly two decades ago, the Batwa lived in the mountain forest of Mgahinga as well as in the deep forest of Bwindi, called the Impenetrable Forest.

In these two places, where a small area of forest is

surrounded by large numbers of poor rural farmers trying to scrape by and live off the land, conservation is a tricky issue.

'It is a question of trying to balance the protection of the forest with the needs of the local communities,' says Alastair McNeilage, from the Wildlife Conservation Society, who works at Bwindi.

When the area was divided into three forest reserves - Mgahinga, Echuya and Bwindi - in the early 1930s, the Batwa stayed where they had been living for generations.

However, when the Ugandan government decided to reinforce the protection of the mountain gorilla habitat, the Batwa were moved from their lands to make way for national parks.

They have become conservation refugees. Anthropologist Chris Sandbrook explains that in the early days of conservation 'local people were excluded from protected areas and kept out with some kind of law enforcement, which has been called fortress conservation.'

Up on a hill, between the Echuya forest and the Bwindi Park, community leader Sembagare Francis recalls:

'One day, we were in the forest when we saw people coming with machine guns and they told us to get out of the forest. We were very scared so we started to run not knowing where to go and some of us disappeared. They either died or went somewhere we didn't know. As a result of the eviction, everybody is now scattered.'

Conservationists, back then, saw local communities as a major threat to wildlife. John Makombo from the Uganda Wildlife Authority says that they aimed to achieve 'sustainable conservation.'

'Originally, when the Batwa were living in the forest they were hunting down all the fauna and that was eradicating almost all the animals: the gorillas were in danger, the chimps were in danger,' Mr Makombo said.

'So, it was not wise to leave [the Batwa] inside the

forest. I think it was better to manage them when they are outside the forest.'

Conservation outcasts

It seems that the Batwa have suffered more than other people from the creation of the parks because they were the people whose livelihoods were most closely related to the forest.

Even now, they tend to be the poorest and most marginalised people who have fewer opportunities to benefit from tourism and other development programmes that have come along with the parks.

They live in unsanitary housing conditions, typically mud huts where the rain comes through.

According to the United Organisation for Batwa Development in Uganda (UOBDU), most are unable to invest in permanent structures as they fear being removed by the owner of the land on which they are squatting.

UOBDU co-ordinator Penninah Zaninka says that the government 'should really think of resettling the Batwa and give them better shelters so that they could benefit from development projects that the government is doing for other citizens of Uganda.'

The government seems to have handed over its responsibility to the few organisations and church groups looking at the plight of the Batwa people.

Minister of State for Tourism Serapio Rukundo told the BBC that it is for 'their future that the government told them to leave the forest.'

He added: 'The question is also: what is the quality of life you would like the Batwa to live? And what rights are you going to guarantee for the animals?'

However, the quality of life of the Batwa does not seem to be taken into account by conservation programmes.

UWA's John Makombo defended their approach: 'Their

conditions of living are not our responsibility. Questions of poverty are not our responsibility.'

Eroding culture

Targeted worldwide by the many tribes evicted from protected areas, big conservation NGOs have now made it clear that they do not support the creation of protected areas that displace indigenous people.

WWF International director general James Leape says mistakes have been made in the past.

'I think that we have, over the last 20 years, learnt case after case that it's a mistake to see conservation and development as opposed to each other. It's clear that we will only be successful in conservation if it works for local communities.'

Nevertheless, hardly any of the staff working for the parks is from the Batwa communities.

'They don't give us a chance to work for the park, when they select people they forget the Batwa,' a member of the Batwa community said.

The Batwa also complain that they cannot access the forest to practice their traditional culture. Most of them fear the park rangers.

'They told us that if anybody goes in the forest to carry out any activities they would be killed,' says Bernard, an elder.

'We have all our traditional equipment here like things to help us collect honey, bows and arrows for hunting - but we haven't taught our children. Even if we wanted to teach them, we can't in this community as we would need to practice in the forest. I'm really not happy that our children cannot learn our culture.'

While their forest-based culture is eroded, the United Nations passed a declaration at the end of last year on the rights of indigenous peoples. It says they cannot be forcibly removed from their lands or territories.

Margaret Lokawua, board member of the UN Permanent Forum on Indigenous Issues, says the Batwa have a case for compensation but it will take some time.

'The Batwa can use this declaration to defend their case and I think they will win; the government will give them a piece of land," she explained.

'But looking at the governments that we have in Africa, it takes time. Meanwhile the Batwa will continue to be squatters on other people's land.'

There may be some hope, but this declaration is non-binding and Uganda was absent when it was adopted." - (Thomas Fessy, "Batwa Face Uncertain Future," BBC World Service, 9 March 2008).

The marginalisation of the Batwa may be the most extreme case in Uganda. But there are other groups which don't get as much attention from the government as the big ones do.

And while it's true that Uganda is composed of many ethnic groups, it's equally true that the history of the country has largely been shaped by only a few of them, especially the ones which had powerful kingdoms or other major centres of power.

Teso

One of these major traditional centres of power – besides Buganda, Bunyoro, Ankole, Toro and Busoga – is Teso.

The people of this area are called Iteso. They are a branch of the eastern Nilotic language speakers and are one of the largest ethnic groups in Uganda.

The eastern branch of Nilotic is divided into the Teso-speaking and Maa-speaking (Maasai) branches. The Teso branch is further divided into speakers of Ateso (the language of the Iteso) and those of the Karamojong cluster including the Turkana, Ikaramojong, Jie, and Dodoth in Kenya and Uganda.

Iteso traditions relate that the Iteso originated somewhere in what is now Sudan and moved south over a period of centuries. But it's not possible to calculate the time of this movement.

A body of Iteso is said to have separated from the Karamojong and moved further south. This may have been a very early separation because the clan names and ritual customs associated with the second of two distinctive groups of Karamojong and Jie people are not found among the Iteso.

Iteso clan names reveal a history of long-standing ethnic interactions. Names of Bantu and Northern Nilotic origin are found among them. And they were probably well-established in their northern Uganda heartland by the mid-1700s when they began to move farther south.

Traditions recorded among the JoPadhola indicate there were two waves of Iteso migration from what's now Sudan.

The first was family-based and peaceful. It was followed by a more extensive and aggressive migration that left the Iteso in control of a large swath of territory that by 1850 extended as far as the western highlands of Kenya.

European travellers record extensive fear of Iteso warriors; nonetheless, the Iteso soon suffered reverses that caused them to draw back to their current territory in Kenya.

Since then, the northern and southern Iteso territories have been separated.

Relations with other societies throughout the precolonial period were alternately peaceful and acrimonious.

And as a result of spatial inter-mixture and intermarriage, Iteso elements and customs can be found among neighbouring peoples and vice versa. Intermarriage has always been extensive.

It is likely that ethnic identity hardened during the colonial period, as it has since, when resources such as land were newly defined as belonging to "tribes."

The Iteso in Kenya and Uganda were conquered by African colonial agents of the British,And the colonial rulers ruled through them indirectly.

What's now western Kenya was transferred from Uganda to Kenya in 1902. As a result, the economic and political histories of the northern Iteso – those in Uganda – and the part of the southern Iteso living in Kenya have taken vastly different courses.

At independence, the Ugandan Iteso were far more wealthy than their Kenyan counterparts. This difference resulted from the status of Uganda as a protectorate reserved for "African development" and western Kenya's status as a labour reserve for the European-owned farms in the "White Highlands."

As a minority people in Kenya, the Iteso are not well-known and have been viewed with some suspicion by surrounding peoples. On the other hand, the Kenyan Iteso have not suffered from the political destabilisation their brethren have in Uganda since 1971 when Amin seized power.

There are profound cultural differences among the Iteso which have regional character and influence. For example, the language of the northern Iteso was extensively influenced by the Baganda who ruled the Iteso under the system of indirect rule. They ruled the Iteso on behalf of the colonial authorities. Southern Iteso, spoken in Kenya, is close to Turkana, lingustic similaries which show profound regional influences and historical ties.

As a result of living among Bantu- and Nilotic-speaking peoples, the southern Iteso have probably been subject to a greater variety of cultural influences.

The Teso territory in northeastern Uganda stretches south from Karamoja into the well-watered region of Lake

Kyoga.

The great majority of Iteso occupy Soroti District and some of the adjacent areas in the north-eastern part of the country. Farther east and south, they constitute about half of the population of Bukedi District. These Iteso are separated from their more northern Ugandan colleagues by Bantu-speaking peoples, notably the Gisu, Banyole, and Bagwere.

They are not separated spatially from the Kenyan Iteso of Busia District in the Western Province, with whom they share a common border

The Iteso of Soroti District, Uganda, are called the northern Iteso in the ethnographic literature; the Iteso of Bukedi District, Uganda, and Busia District, Kenya, are called the southern Iteso.

The southern Iteso occupy the foothills of Mount Elgon and the surrounding savanna. The northern Iteso environment varies from low and wet near the shores of Lake Kyoga and its neighboring swamps to high and arid in the north.

In both areas, annual rainfall is separated into two wet seasons – the "short" and "long" rains. It varies considerably from year to year and locality to locality.

The Iteso have always moved their households in response to changes in economy, politics, and climate. After the 1950s, land scarcity and colonial (later state) control prevented the Iteso from adapting their economy to the environment. And their population in the more arid parts of northern Uganda is sparse and small.

They're basically farmers but they also own cattle and other livestock. Originally they were cattle herders like the Karamojong but not strictly pastoralist.

Unlike the other Teso-speaking ethnic groups, the Iteso have never been transhumant or nomadic; agriculture has played as significant a role in their social, economic, and expressive lives as cattle have among the other groups. But recent cattle raids by the Karamojong – who use

85

automatic weapons including AK 47s – have resulted in a sharp decline in cattle ownership among the Iteso.

In fact, the situation has deteriorated so badly in recent years that many people in the northern regions of the Teso territory have been forced to move to camps for displaced people fearing nigh-time raids by the Karamojong.

The civil strife intensified through the years especially since the mid-1980s.

But the conflict in Teso territory in northeastern Uganda was not ignited by cattle rustling. It's true the Karamojong cattle rustlers unleashed terror among the Teso. However, the main culprit was a rebel group known as the Uganda People's Army.

It was based in Teso and started its insurgency against the government in 1987, about a year after Museveni seized power from President Obote. The group was opposed to Museveni's rule and was active between 1987 and 1992.

The conflict was also ethnic – mostly Teso and Nilotic, while most of the national leaders under Museveni were Bantu and southerners. Therefore the conflict also had an ethnic and regional dimension. The Teso supported Obote, a fellow Nilotic and fellow northerner.

The insurgency caused a lot of suffering among the Teso before it ended through mediation.

The Teso have been successful farmers for a long time unlike some of their neighbours. Even those who suffered during the war when their homeland was the battleground between the rebels and government forces have shown a remarkable degree of endurance. And many of them are successful farmers today as much as they were before the war.

Many Tesos joined Uganda's cash economy when coffee and cotton were introduced in 1912 and the region has thrived through agriculture and commerce.

Traditionally, the Iteso lived in settlements consisting of scattered homesteads, each organised around a stockade and several granaries. And they still do so today, although with modernisation many also live independently while others have moved to urban centres in other parts of Uganda. They are urbanised like the Baganda, although not to the same extent.

Groups of homesteads are united around a hearth where men who form the core of the settlement gather for ritual and social purposes.

The groups usually consist of patrilineally related males whose wives, children and other relatives form the remainder of the settlement.

Several groups constitute a clan. Clans are loosely organised but clan elders maintain ritual observances in honour of their ancestors. However, such observances should not be construed as ancestor worship.

The Teso don't worship their departed ancestors but see them as intermediaries who intercede with God on their behalf; a common belief in many traditional African religions.

The Supreme Being is called *Edeke* in the Teso language.

Traditionally, the Teso believe that ancestral spirits bring bad luck if they are not appeased.

Every family had a shrine where libations were often poured or placed to placate the ancestors. And the practice is still common among many people who follow the traditional religion.

Western influence has had an impact in changing those beliefs. But even a significant number of people who have been converted to Christianity still believe in the power of their ancestors and their influence on the living.

Men of the clan consult the elders about social customs, especially marriage, and rituals.

Many of their customs are not unique in the region because of intermingling with members of other ethnic groups and shared history. The Teso share many cultural traits with the Langi, one of the largest ethnic groups in northern Uganda and in the country.

They have been influenced by the Karamojong who are their Nilotic brethren, and by Bantu groups especially the Basoga who, in turn, have been heavily influenced by the Baganda and the Banyoro.

There is also a clear division of labour in Teso society as is the case in many traditional societies in Uganda and other parts of Africa.

Much of the agricultural work is done by women. Women may also own land and granaries. But after the introduction of cash crops, most of the land was claimed by men and passed on to their sons.

Separation between men and women is also strictly enforced traditionally. Men and women don't eat together. They eat separately, a custom I have also observed among members of different ethnic groups including the Nyakyusa of southwestern Tanzania. Even modernised Africans from many different ethnic groups strictly enforce this custom, including those who live in cities.

The Teso also have strict taboos. Traditionally, women did not eat chicken the same way women didn't among the Toro.

There are a number of other animals even Teso men were not allowed to eat. For example, the bush-buck – called *ederet* in the Teso language – was taboo for many clans.

It's still a male-dominated society and little has changed in terms of relations between men and women in spite of the influence of modernisation which has reached even some of the most remote parts of Uganda in varying degrees.

All Teso men within a settlement, related and unrelated, are organised on the basis of age.

The Teso are basically conservative and stick to tradition probably more than many other groups in Uganda. But also, like many other people of the Kenya-Uganda border region, they have a history of extensive multi-ethnic contact and have come to share many customs with neighbouring peoples, although not at the expense of their identity or cultural distinctiveness.

The Teso of Uganda have also been been described as being among the most economically adaptable people. And in remarkable contrast, their brethren across the border in Kenya have an undeserved reputation for cultural conservatism. They are probably no more conservative than the Teso of Uganda.

Although all the major traditional kingdoms are located in southern Uganda, the northern part of the country is not without its share of attractions including major ethnic groups and traditional institutions.

Lango

Besides the Teso, the Acholi and the Lango are the other main groups in northern Uganda.

Strictly speaking, the Teso are a northeastern group, therefore still northern but not typical northern like the Acholi and the Lango

The Lango are sometimes called Langi. Their language is also called Lango. They live in Lango, a sub-region in north-central Uganda north of Lake Kyoga.

Their language is Luo and is mutually intelligible with Acholi (which is also Luo). It is related to other Luo languages in Uganda and Kenya.

It's a western Nilotic language like those of the Acholi and the Alur who are their northern neighbours. But the Lango also share many cultural traits with the Ateker, their neighbours to the east and who are classified as eastern Nilotic.

When the Lango migrated to the region from the northeast – Sudan and some anthropologists claim from Ethiopia – they found the Acholi who had arrived there earlier, also from the north, and intermingled with them.

Because of their long interaction with the Acholi, the Lango lost their Ateker language and adopted Luo spoken by their Acholi neighbours.

The situation is similar to what happened in Ruanda-Urundi (Rwanda and Burundi) where the Tutsi – who migrated from the north – also lost their original language after intermingling with the Hutu and adopted the language of the people they had conquered.

In fact, in the case of Uganda, some Langos identify with the Luo.

But in spite of their linguistic affiliation with other Luo speakers, the vast majority of the Lango reject the "Luo" label. They say they're not Luo.

Some historians believe the Lango represent the descendants of 15th century dissenters from Karamojong society to the east.

Lango society is organised into localised patrilineages and further grouped into clans which are dispersed throughout the territory.

Clan members claim descent from a common ancestor. But they are seldom able to recount the nature of their relationship to the clan founder.

They have been well-organised as a society for centuries, although not as complex as the Bantu kingdoms of southern Uganda.

Originally, the Langi – or Lango – were pastoralists but they later became farmers.

They ate meat and drank milk. And their economy was based on barter. They used to barter cattle, goats and grains with the Acholi, the Labwor, and the Kumam and later, with the Arabs. But as they continued to move towards Lake Kyoga, they abandoned their pastoral economy.

But they still own livestock. So they are both "pastoral" and agricultural – except that they now live in permanent settlements instead of moving from place to place as typical pastoralists do, traversing vast expanses of territory in search of pasture.

Their main crop is millet. They also rely on animal husbandry for subsistence. In some areas, people also cultivate maize, eleusine, peanuts, sesame seed, sweet potatoes, and cassava.

They also grow and eat simsim which was introduced by the colonial government in 1911.

When they first started farming, their first food crops were millet, peas and others. They later started to grow groundnuts and sweet potatoes which were introduced form Bunyoro.

Both Lango and Acholi generally assign agricultural tasks either to men or women. In many cases, men are responsible for cattle while women work in the fields.

In some villages, only adult men may milk cows.

An Acholi or Lango man may marry more than one wife, but he may not marry within his lineage or that of his mother. A woman lives in her husband's homestead which may include his brothers and their families. Each wife has a separate house and hearth for cooking.

Many of these cultural practices and customs are shared by other Nilotic groups in northern Uganda, although some of them are unique to the Lango.

Acholi

The most prominent ethnic group in northern Uganda is not the Langi but the Acholi. The Langi are second to the Acholi in terms of prominence in northern Uganda.

The Acholi are also one of the most well-known ethnic groups in Uganda and in the entire East Africa.

They speak Luo as their native language.

Their homeland is the former Acholi District – now divided into the Gulu and Kitgum districts – and the adjoining area of southern Sudan. Most of them live in Uganda.

The Acholi landscape is characterised by rolling grasslands with scattered trees, streams, and rock outcrops. Northern Uganda is usually drier and less fertile than the south. The dry season is long and hot and the Acholi have adapted to this harsh environment.

Most Acholis are farmers – or peasants. Their man crops include millet, sorghum,beans, various kinds of peas, maize, cassava, vegetables, groundnuts, simsim (sesame), fruits and cotton.

The most common domestic animals are – and have long been – chickens and goats, with some cattle, especially in the dryer portions of Acholi.

Men have traditionally played a significant role in agriculture, especially for such time-limited, labour-intensive tasks as clearing, planting, and harvesting, often as part of lineage-based cooperative labour teams.

Women also work in the fields. They're also responsible for most child rearing, all cooking and other food-preparation tasks.

The building of houses and granaries has historically involved both men and women, with each performing specified functions.

Boys and girls are typically socialised into distinct gender roles and do household and other chores accordingly.

Since the advent of colonial rule, an average of 10 to 20 per cent of adult Acholi males at any one time have been involved in migrant labour or employment in the police or army that has taken them from their home and families – mostly to the south.

But only a small number of Acholis have filled middle-level or senior civil-service positions in independent Uganda. Most of these jobs are taken by southerners who are, relatively speaking, far more educated than their northern counterparts are.

The situation is reminiscent of what happened in Nigeria where northerners – especially the Hausa – also joined the army during colonial rule and after independence in disproportionately large numbers as riflemen, while better educated southerners, mostly Igbos and the Yorubas, served as army officers and as civil servants.

The neighbours of the Acholi include the Luo-speaking Langi, Paluo, and Alur to the south and southwest, the central Sudanic-speaking Madi to the west, and the eastern Nilotic Jie and Karamojong to the east.

One of the main reasons why the Acholi are so prominent in Ugandan contemporary history is that they joined the army in very large numbers and virtually dominated the armed forces as did other northerners.

Although the Acholi constituted less than 5 per cent of Uganda's population during the early years of independence, they were disproportionately represented in the army. An entire third of the enlisted men in the Ugandan army were Acholi. And more than 15 per cent of the police force were also Acholi.

Their dominant role in the armed forces also enabled them to play a major role in Uganda's political life.

But their prominence in Uganda's security forces – army, intelligence, and air force – has also been a curse, sometimes, in a country wracked by violence. The violence has been fuelled by ethnic rivalries and the Acholi have been at the centre of this maelstrom in a number of conflicts.

Traditionally, the Acholi have been ruled by chiefs for centuries. Chiefdoms consisted of a number of fenced villages, each with recognised land rights vested in the patrilineal lineage – known as *kaka* – at its core.

Lineage heads, assisted by lineage elders, organised production based on cooperative village-lineage labour; controlled marriage; oversaw rituals and were the main advisors to the chief. They were also responsible for most of the social control exercised in Acholi.

But through the decades, chiefdoms in Acholi have

93

become vestigial institutions, and the fences that once enclosed villages have disappeared.

Most Acholi, however, continue to live in neighbourhoods – parishes – that not only consist predominantly of patrilineal kinsmen and their wives but often carry the old lineage names.

Most Acholi also continue to live in thatched, round mud houses, although wealthier ones and those who live in towns or near major roads have square houses of mud or block with iron or tile roofs.

Extensive mission activity in Acholiland by both Protestants and Catholics has attracted many followers since the second decade of the 20th century, bringing about fundamental change in the lives of many people in that part of Uganda.

But in spite of all that, traditional beliefs still persist and are often meshed with Christian doctrine in complex ways. One illustration of this is the various spirit-possession-based millennial – and military – movements that have been prominent in Acholi during the extremely difficult period of the late 1980s and early 1990s, most famously the Holy Spirit Movement of Alice Lakwena.

The Lord's Resistance Army (LRA) led by John Kony, a cousin of the late Alice Lakwena, was the most brutal manifestation of these kinds of religious beliefs which are also expressed by military means. Kony claimed he spoke with angels and wanted Uganda to be ruled on the basis of the Ten Commandments.

Appendix

The Swahili and their culture

THE SWAHILI are found mostly in Kenya and Tanzania along the coast. They are also found in urban centres in other parts of both countries but not in large numbers as they are in the coastal regions. And they are mostly Muslim.

Although the Swahili people, or Waswahili as they are known in the Kiswahili language, are considered to be de-tribalized Africans, members of tribes indigenous to the coast are also considered to be Waswahili.

One of the best examples is the Zaramo, or Wazaramo, in Tanzania who are the original inhabitants of Dar es Salaam, the former capital which is now the commercial capital although in most cases it is still the capital city of Tanzania. Even the president of Tanzania still lives in Dar es Salaam, not in Dodoma in the hinterland which is the official capital.

The Swahili have lived along the coast for centuries, probably since 100 A.D. There were African tribes along the coast and when the Arabs came, they interacted and intermarried with the indigenous people. The product of this intermingling was the Swahili people and Swahili culture.

Therefore most of the people who are called Swahili or Waswahili are a mixed group of people, racially with the Arabs, and in terms of inter-tribal marriage of coastal tribes who were from the beginning strongly influenced by the Arabs and adopted Islam and Arab culture.

Persians, especially in what is Tanzania today, contributed to the evolution of the swahili and Swahilu culture. They came mostly from a region called Shiraz in Persia, Iran today, and their descendants who intermarried with Africans still live in Zanzibar today. They are also found in other parts of Tanzania and even in Kenya.

Marriage between Arabs and Africans, and between Persians and Africans, was one-sided in the sense it was Arab and Persian men who married black African women. It was unthinkable for African men to marry Arab women or Persian women. And the intermarriage was mostly between Arabs and Africans. Persians who settled in East Africa were far fewer than the Arabs who migrated to the region through the centuries.

What is also important to remember is that there was no Islam before the prophet Mohammed. Yet there were Arabs who settled who settled in East Africa long before Islam, and long before Mohammed was born.

Therefore evolution of Swahili culture - a product of intermingling and intermarriage between Arabs and Africans - started before the advent and propagation of Islam but was reinforced centuries later with the spread of the Islamic faith. And the Swahili people themselves came into being before Islam since racial intermarriage between Arabs and Africans started taking place centuries before Islam became a religion.

It was not until the 700s A.D. that Islam was introduced to East Africa after prophet Mohammed died in 632 A.D. It was also during that period that Arabs started settling in East Africa in large numbers, many of them spreading the Islamic faith.

But while Swahilisation of the East African coast and evolution of the Swahili culture preceded Islam, Islam did, centuries later especially since the 700s A.D., profoundly influence Swahili culture and in fact virtually transformed it into Islamic culture, clearly demonstrated even today on the East African coast where almost all the Swahili people are Muslims, or Moslems, whichever term they prefer to use.

What is also important to remember is that it was not just those who were the product of inter-racial marriage between Arabs and Africans who became or were considered to be Swahili people together with de-tribalised Africans and tribal Africans who had adopted Swahili culture. Arabs themselves also became Swahili, or Waswahili, just like their black counterparts and those of mixed race.

And even today, Arabs in Kenya and Tanzania are called - and consider themselves to be – Waswahili. The Swahili identity transcends race.

Most of the Arabs in Kenya and Tanzania speak Swahili, or Kiswahili, as their mother-tongue although they are also bilingual and speak Arabic as well.

Even many Swahili people who have African and Arab ancestry also speak Arabic although Kiswahili is their native language as much as it is for de-tribalised black Africans who don't know their tribal languages.

Tanzania has more people whose mother-tongue is Kiswahili than Kenya does. But Kenya also has some Waswahili, especially those in Mombasa and Lamu, who are more "typical Swahili" than many Swahili people in Tanzania.

One of them is renowned Kenyan scholar, Professor Ali Mazrui from Mombasa, who is both black African and Arab in terms of racial heritage, as many people along the East African coast are. As he has emphatically stated on a number of occasions, Kiswahili is his mother-tongue, or

97

his native language. But he also speaks Arabic. And he is a Muslm.

He is a typical Swahili – in spite of being Westernised in terms of education and lifestyle – and has the following to say about the Swahili people and the Swahili culture in one of his lectures:

Uswahili International:
Between Language and Cultural Synthesis

Professor Ali A. Mazrui

Delivered at Fort Jesus, Mombasa, Kenya on July 19, 2005, as part of the launch of the Swahili Resource Centre, Coastal Branch, Kenya.

The event was also a commemoration of the works of Sheikh Al-Amin Aly Mazrui, the late Chief Kadhi of Kenya who was also the father of the future professor, Ali Mazrui, who was 14 years old when his father died in 1947 at the age of 58.

This Resource Centre is primarily focused on Swahili culture, rather than the Swahili language.

Is there a Swahili culture apart from the language? A culture is a way of life of a people.

In order for there to be a distinct Swahili culture, there has to be a distinct Swahili people. Is there a Swahili people with a distinct way of life of its own?

The Swahili people are those who originated the Swahili language. They themselves emerged at the Coast of Kenya and Tanzania; they were originally overwhelmingly Muslim and they had strong cultural links with Coastal African tribes, on the one hand, and the Arabian peninsular, on the other.

Like medieval Islam, Swahili culture was enhanced by a spirit of *creative synthesis*. Islamic civilization was at its best when it was prepared to learn from other cultures and civilizations.

In mathematics ancient Islamic civilization was stimulated by India. In philosophy Islamic civilization was stimulated by ancient Greeks. In architecture Islamic civilization was stimulated by pre-Islamic Persia. In asylum and political refuge early Muslims enjoyed the protection of Africans in the Horn of Africa.

During the lifetime of the Prophet Muhammad himself, Arab Muslims were being persecuted by pre-Islamic Arabs on the Arabian peninsular. A group of endangered Arab Muslims crossed the Red Sea into Abyssinia (now called Ethiopia) in search of political asylum and religious refuge.

They were protected by an African Christian monarch. Among the refugees was Uthman bin Affan, later destined to become the third Caliph of Islam and the protector of the Qur'an.

Islamic civilization subsequently declined when it became less and less ready to learn from other civilizations, and condemned major cultural changes as bid'a - that is, as dangerous innovations.

Like ancient Islamic civilization, Swahili culture initially prospered through a spirit of *creative synthesis* – ready to learn from other cultures.

While the basic foundation of the Kiswahili language was Bantu African, the language quite early demonstrated readiness to borrow extensively from Arabic.

Sometimes the configuration of Arabic and Bantu African concepts constituted a remarkable balancing act.

Bantu:
Kusini na Kaskazini – North and South
Arabic:
Mashariki na Magharibi – East and West
Bantu:
Uchumi – Economics

Arabic:
Siasa – Politics
Bantu:
Bunge – Parliament
Arabic:
Raisi – President
Bantu:
Balozi – Ambassador
Arabic:
Waziri – Minister
Bantu:
Chumvi (or Munyu) – Salt
Arabic:
Sukari – Sugar
Bantu:
Mungu – God
Arabic:
Angel – Malaika
Bantu:
Nguvu – Strength
Arabic:
Afya – Health
Bantu:
Utumwa – Slavery
Arabic:
Uhuru – Freedom
Bantu:
Mjomba – Maternal Uncle
Arabic:
Ami – Paternal Uncle
Bantu:
Shangazi – Paternal Aunt
Arabic:
Khalati – Maternal Aunt
Bantu:
Nyama – Meat
Arabic:

Samaki – Fish
Bantu:
Mto – River
Arabic:
Bahari – Ocean or Sea
Bantu:
Moja, Mbili, Tatu. Nne, Tano – One, Two, Three, Four, Five
Arabic:
Sita, Saba, Tisa – Six, Seven, Nine
Bantu:
Kumi – Ten
Arabic:
Ishirini mpaka Mia – Twenty to a Hundred

In interacting with both Arab and Indian civilizations, Swahili architecture and systems of decoration were affected.

Elaborately carved Lamu doors, copper decorated chests, ivory decorated Lamu thrones, entered Swahili decorative worlds – as well as beautiful copper coffee pots and the small coffee cups.

In the creative synthesis Swahili culture helped to Africanize the tabla (Indian drum) for events which have ranged from tarabu (Swahili concert) to maulidi (celebrating the Prophet's birthday), alongside matari (dancing drums with small bells attached).

Arabic music also provided the ud to Swahili culture – an Arabian Nights guitar.

The Swahili flute was influenced by both Middle Eastern and South Asian orchestration.

Creative synthesis also incorporated into Kiswahili several food cuisines. Swahili cuisine seeks to incorporate such South Asian dishes as pilau, biriani, and chapatti – none of which are identical with the Indian varieties.

Some of the spices carry Arab names rather than Indian – such as bizari for curry powder and thumu or thomo for

101

garlic.

Swahili architecture in places like Lamu and the ruins of Gedi continue to reflect this responsiveness to the cultures of other societies.

This Fort Jesus was built by the Portuguese. It was from time to time Swahilized, especially when the rulers of Mombasa were for a while either Swahilized Arabs or Arabized Waswahili.

The Portuguese brought maize to East Africa. Most Europeans at the time called maize "Indian corn".

The word "Indian" refers to Americo-Indians (Red Indians, rather than Hindustan).

To the present day, the name for maize in Kiswahili is hindi (singular) or mahindi (plural). A salute to Montezuma, the Emperor of Mexico.

Words we have borrowed from Portuguese include the big one – pesa, meaning money. It is borrowed from pesos, the Iberian currency.

Other Portuguese words: sapatu (slippers), shimizi (female undergarment), kandirinya (water kettle).

The Germans gave Kiswahili such educational words as shule (school). The Arabs gave us elimu (scholarly knowledge), the Africans gave us chuo and chuo kikuu (educational institution and university), and the British gave us words which range from profesa to sayansi, from baiskeli to dimokrasi, and from manuwari (man of war – or battleship) to sinema (cinema).

This readiness to respond to other cultures and languages makes Kiswahili very similar to the English language. Both languages have been spectacularly successful. English words which the British have borrowed from Arabic include algebra, tariff (from taarifa), admiral (from emir), and, surprisingly, alcohol (al-quhl).

The most famous English loan word borrowed from Kiswahili is the word safari. In English the word means "hunting trip in Africa" – though in Swahili usage safari refers to any kind of travelling.

Kiswahili borrowed the word from Arabic and then loaned the word to the English language. *Creative synthesis* in all its intricate interconnections.

We must conclude that although the Swahili language is the legacy of words, the Swahili culture is a much wider phenomenon – including marriage customs, the traditions of child rearing, cuisine, architecture, dress code.

Kiswahili has greatly influenced neighboring African languages. The kanzu in Kenya is associated with Swahili culture, and most wearers of the kanzu in Kenya are Muslims.

The kanzu in Uganda is not associated with any religion. The Kabaka of Buganda – a leading member of the Anglican global community – often wears the kanzu on ceremonial Christian occasions.

The word for religion in Luganda is dini. "Dini" also serves the same purpose in a large number of other East African indigenous languages.

Today we start an enterprise about Swahili culture as a whole. We have also honored Sheikh Al-Amin Aly Mazrui because he was one of the most influential writers of the Swahili language and a major expert of the manners, customs and beliefs of the Waswahili.

May this enterprise be blessed by our ancestors, supported by our people, served by our community, protected by our government and helped to grow to full maturity and triumph by the Almighty God. Amen.

Kila tunapomsheherekea mtu mwema, huwa na sisi tuna wema ndani ya nyoyo zetu.

An American playwright [John Drinkwater] has captured the same spirit in the following words about Abraham Lincoln:

When the high heart we magnify,

103

And the sure vision celebrate,
And worship greatness passing by,
Ourselves are great.

On a day like this I am proud and grateful that my father's high heart has been magnified, his sure vision celebrated, and his greatness suitably recognized.

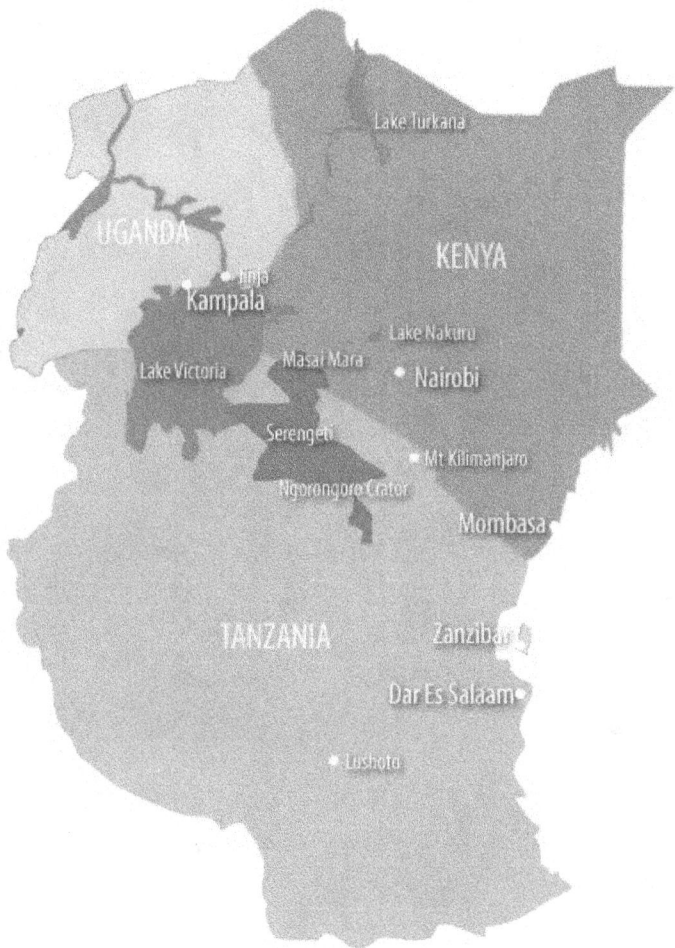

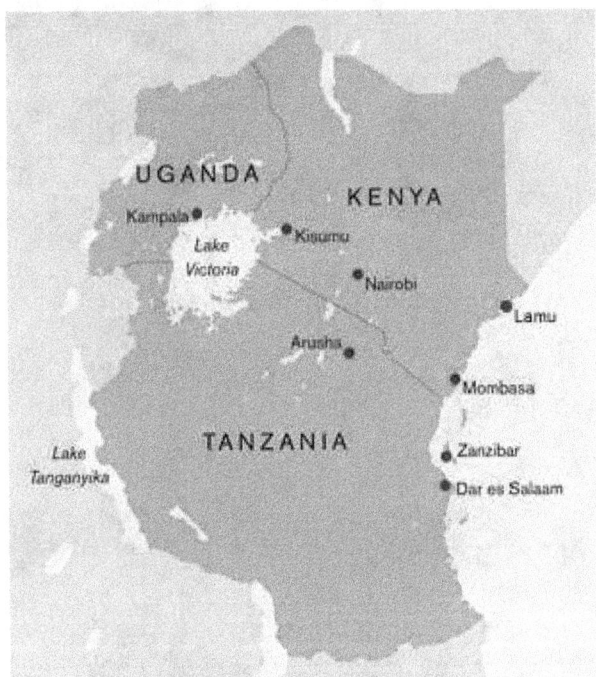

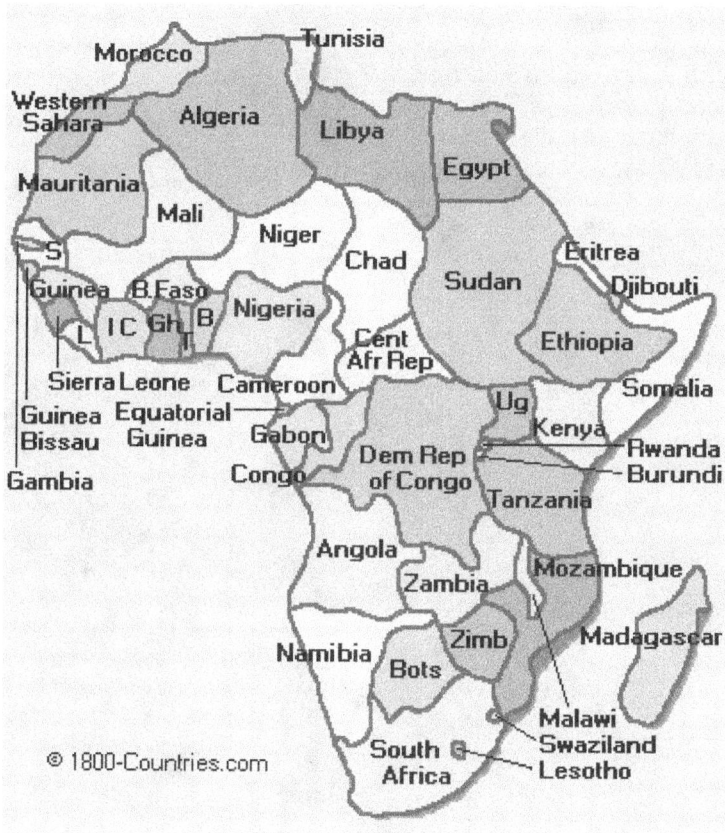

Morocco
Tunisia
Western Sahara
Algeria
Libya
Egypt
Mauritania
Mali
Niger
Chad
Eritrea
Sudan
Djibouti
S
Guinea
B.Faso
Nigeria
Cent Afr Rep
Ethiopia
L
I C
Gh
B
Sierra Leone
Cameroon
Somalia
Guinea Bissau
Equatorial Guinea
Gabon
Ug
Kenya
Gambia
Congo
Dem Rep of Congo
Rwanda
Burundi
Tanzania
Angola
Zambia
Mozambique
Namibia
Zimb
Madagascar
Bots
Malawi
South Africa
Swaziland
Lesotho

© 1800-Countries.com